CHRISTIAN LEADERSHIP

50 Stories that Connect Faith and Everyday Life

Terry L. Sumerlin

Christian Leadership: 50 Stories that Connect Faith and Everyday Life
©Terry L. Sumerlin, 2017

First Printing 2017
Printed in the United States of America

Published by:
S E Publishing
P.O. Box 796601
Dallas, TX 75379

ISBN:
print: 978-0-9659662-6-9
ebook: 978-0-9659662-7-6

Cover Artist: Aundrea Hernandez

Table of Contents

PROLOGUE

A church sign said, "God wants spiritual fruit, not religious nuts." If I am a nut, I'm a nut whether I'm a Christian or not. However, I am a Christian.

If that statement offends you in some way, I'm sorry. I'm not sorry that I'm a Christian. I'm sorry that there might be a barrier between us. I think we would like each other, and that you would like my book.

I became a Christian when I was eleven years old. At that age I began (to the best of my young ability) to follow Jesus. When I was twenty-one I became what is sometimes called a pulpit minister or a full-time preacher. I served churches in that capacity for about twenty-five years. Now I'm a full-time conference speaker and writer. I also remain very active in the church where my wife and I are members.

Sometimes I'm asked how I got into professional speaking. Though I did not become a preacher with a view to that being a stepping stone toward professional speaking, the skills are related. However, I honed my speaking skills and developed a keen interest in motivation and leadership as an instructor for a well-known public speaking and human relations course.

I recall that at the end of an intensive ten days of training to become an instructor for that course, the trainer called me into his office where he told me I had passed muster. But he had a question for me. "Can you instruct this course," he asked, "without sounding like a preacher?" I told him I thought I could.

Since then, I've had occasion to think many times about his question. It's a question I often ask myself as a conference speaker. It's also a question that those in pulpits would do well to ask themselves. People don't want to be preached to. Nowadays, a dignified, conversational style works best for every type of presentation.

It also works best for books. For that reason, you won't find this book to be preachy or judgmental. What you will find is a book that contains anecdotes that illustrate truths expressed in Biblical passages. The stories are related to inform, entertain, encourage, inspire, and provoke thought regarding how Christians are to effectively lead and positively influence others. What is discussed is not rocket science or stodgy theory. It's Main-Street-type common sense.

The type of leadership that is illustrated in these anecdotes is the same type that I address in conferences of all types and sizes, from St. Paul to St. Thomas and from the British Isles to the island of Guam. It's positive influence. It's the kind of positive influence that is required for successful corporate executives and organizational heads. But it's also required and attainable for those who may not be suited for or desire leadership positions, yet they interact daily with others.

Christians are expected to be the salt of the earth and the light of the world. That's what Jesus taught.

Following Jesus every day in everything we do, say, and think is what this book is about. How doing so positively impacts the lives of others is what leadership is about. My prayer is that this book will inspire each of us to be a blessing to everyone, every day, in every way—because we desire to please the Lord.

DEDICATION

To Paul H. Smith, my longtime editor extraordinaire, mentor, and esteemed friend, who so ably demonstrates the principles discussed in this book. My life is richer for knowing you!

Section One: Self-Improvement

Every action and interaction is the result of how we think.

Therefore, however you want people to treat you, so treat them, for this is the Law and the Prophets.
– Matthew 7:12

THE GOLD STANDARD

Both the religious and non-religious have heard of the Golden Rule. It is a paraphrase of Jesus' words and is quoted by many: "Do unto others as you would have others do unto you."

Most have also heard the crass interpretation of the rule that says, "The man who has the gold makes the rules."

Actually, the rule is called golden for much better reasons. In dealing with others and with respect to how the rule impacts our lives, its value is as gold. Yet, few seem to really understand it, and even fewer apply it.

I pointed these things out one morning when I gave a brief chapel talk at Florida College, a religiously oriented liberal arts college that I attended forty-six years ago. I was third in my class. Third from the bottom!

On the same occasion, I was privileged to kick off their annual Enrichment Series with a presentation on leadership. Both were exciting opportunities for me.

In the chapel talk, I connected the two presentations by saying, "Effective leadership is positive influence — the Golden Rule at its best." Then I discussed for a few minutes what the Golden Rule is and isn't and how it would tie into my evening leadership presentation. Following are a few things I pointed out.

For certain, the principle involves something better than returning meanness for meanness, rudeness for rudeness, or injury for injury. Yet, we somehow tend to feel justified in personal or business relationships when we mistreat those who have mistreated us. In response to such, we might simply ask, "How's that working for you?"

Your response might be, "It sure doesn't work as well as when I'm nice to others." Indeed! Yet, in light of this, we sometimes misconstrue the rule to mean that we should simply repay kindness with kindness. And, that's certainly an improvement over rudeness for rudeness. However, it doesn't require much of us. Most can be nice to those who are nice to them.

"Well," one says, "I think I apply the Golden Rule by being a completely harmless person. I wouldn't deliberately hurt anyone." That's great! The world certainly has plenty of room for harmless people.

But, the Golden Rule is proactive. It's not what we don't do. It's what we do. And what we do, if we do what Jesus taught, is treat others as we would like to be treated — without regard for what another has done to us or for us and without regard for future repayment,

Tough to apply? You bet! In fact, oftentimes my failure in applying the rule disappoints me. But, we must keep trying, because the benefits are well worth the effort. Though it's a rare person who truly understands the rule and consistently applies it in every relationship, that individual is generally rich in friendships, relationships, health, and happiness.

LEADERSHIP TIP: Enrich your life by going for the gold in all relationships.

Finally, brethren, whatever is true, whatever is honorable, whatever is right, whatever is pure, whatever is lovely, whatever is of good report, if there is any excellence and if anything worthy of praise, let your mind dwell on these things.
– Philippians 4:8

WHAT DO YOU THINK?

I enjoy thinking. In fact, perhaps sometimes I think too much. Too often I prefer reading and thinking over socializing and interacting.

The fact that I like to think doesn't mean I think I'm a profound thinker or that I'm always correct in my thinking. I just like to think.

Perhaps you're also a thinker. If so, you're a better leader as a result. Your ideas are fresher, your vision better, and your enthusiasm greater. You've likely discovered things that enhance your thinking as well as things that diminish it. Let's see if we're on the same page.

Good thinking requires that one occasionally be different. Emerson said, "Whoso would be a man, must be a nonconformist." The same is true of a man or woman who thinks mature thoughts.

This does not demand that one be different just for the sake of being different. Such would be like the fellow who, for the sake of being different, decided to part his hair from ear to ear rather than from front to back. Finally, he decided to conform—because he got tired of people whispering in his nose.

By nonconformist I'm simply suggesting that one acquire both the ability to think outside the box and the courage to accept proper conclusions. However, it seems that a requirement for this would be to first know what's in the box. Otherwise, one tips his hand to the fact that he just wants to be different.

Another requirement for good thinking is good reading. Booker T. Washington observed: "In my contact with people I find that, as a rule, it is only the little, narrow people who live for themselves, who never read good books, who do not travel, who never open up their souls in a way to permit them to come into contact with other souls—with the great outside world." Just as surely as conversation with various individuals can make us think, as well as broaden our minds, good reading serves the same purpose.

Unfortunately, too many are not readers and many who are read the wrong things. What are the right things? Though the Bible would certainly be at the top of the list, I'm certainly not the authority as relates to secular reading material. However, I can say that if we always read from those with whom we agree we'll never know the excitement and satisfaction of having new thoughts.

Effective thinkers (and leaders) read or listen to those who challenge their thoughts. That produces good thinking—growth! Motivational speaker, Charlie "Tremendous" Jones, was known for saying: "The difference between who you are today and who you will be in five years will be the people you spend time with and the books you read."

Along with nonconformity and spending time with good thinkers (via what we read and hear), good thinking also requires time alone. We spend so much of our time in close proximity of others that, as Emerson said, "You would think the value of man is in his skin." Sometimes we value others more when we have time to ourselves. We also think better that way.

We don't always have to have people around. Nor do we always have to have music or the latest technology. What we generally must have for good thinking is a high enough regard for ourselves that we actually enjoy our own company in solitude. It's a sign of maturity—and good thinking!

LEADERSHIP TIP: We are what we think, but not necessarily what we think we are.

The things you have learned and received and heard and seen in me, practice these things; and the God of peace shall be with you.
– Philippians 4:9

A SURE WAY TO CHANGE YOUR LIFE

If you were asked, "What is the most life-changing thing you have ever learned?", what would be your answer? Mine would be motion changes emotion.

My first exposure to this concept was in something I read many years ago from the father of American psychology, William James. He said: "Action seems to follow feeling, but really action and feeling go together; and by regulating the action, which is under the more direct control of the will, we can indirectly regulate the feeling, which is not." As a practical illustration of this concept, James said that though it is often true that we sing because we are happy, it is also true that we can make ourselves happy by singing. So it is with numerous matters of the mind.

Every day, you and I encounter those who, by their actions and words, choose to make themselves happy or unhappy, enthused or unenthused, miserable or fulfilled. We experience such in our own lives.

The bad news is that we cannot merely think our way out of negative states of mind and into positive ones. The good news is that we can act our way out. However, it means getting off our "buts" and doing something. So, let's look at some things we can do that work a lot better than excuses when it comes to improving our attitudes.

First, we can laugh. Have you noticed that folks seldom laugh out loud anymore? Have you also noticed how many people seem to be unhappy or how many say things to indicate that they are miserable?

Personally, I like to laugh, and I like to make others laugh. However, like everyone else, I occasionally have downer times. These typically occur the day after a speech, when the adrenaline has worn off.

During those times and various other low times, it helps me to take action. This involves taking the focus off self and looking outward—to life and to others.

People and life are funny! But those whose thoughts are turned inward never notice. As a result, they seldom laugh and are often unhappy.

If you're thinking that such folks would laugh were it not for the fact they are unhappy, remember William James' illustration about singing. He said singing can be both cause and effect with respect to happiness. So also can laughter.

Knowing the preceding, I've made it a point to laugh out loud on a regular basis. At night Sherry can sometimes hear me laughing loudly at something I've heard on an old TV comedy. During the day, I often say things to Sherry that I think are funny. If she doesn't think so (or is laughing inwardly), I usually try to strengthen my case by adding, "That was really funny." Even if she still doesn't think so, such words nonetheless positively affect me (and let me know not to use that particular line in a speech!).

My point is, we'll never get happy just by determining to change our thoughts. It takes a change in words and actions.

Enthusiasm works the same way. If we act enthusiastically, then an enthusiastic state of mind will result.

One of the most enthusiastic people I know also happens to be one of the most successful. Though in his 80s, he still walks like he's going to a fire. He greets others as if he hasn't seen them in years. He's interested in everyone and everything and is a fascinating conversationalist.

I believe the same thing might someday be said of my friend, Bartell, that was said concerning the passing of Theodore Roosevelt: "Death had to take him sleeping, for if Roosevelt had been awake there would have been a fight."

Might such, someday, be said of you or me? It is so easy to be unhappy, unenthusiastic, and miserable. All we have to do is talk and act that way, and such will cause and perpetuate that state of mind. On the other hand, if we laugh easily, talk positively, greet others warmly, walk briskly, and live actively, we can't help but have better attitudes and lives.

LEADERSHIP TIP: Change your life by changing your thoughts. Change your thoughts by changing your words and actions.

Brethren, do not be children in your thinking; yet in evil be babes, but in your thinking be mature.
— *1 Corinthians 14:20*

HOW MATURE ARE WE?

"One of the most dangerous things in the world is a ten-year-old mind in a fifty-year-old body." I don't know where I first read that, but I like it! It refers to something that we often witness. Often those who are mature physically, intellectually, or financially are immature emotionally and relationally. In dealing with others, they not only don't get it, they apparently are never going to get it! As a result, they do a great deal of harm to others.

All of this raises the question: How do we know if we are mature where it counts most? What are a few sure signs of emotional and relational maturity or a lack thereof?

It would seem that one indication of maturity is found in *the way we talk*. Are we constantly "me deep" in conversation by either boasting or complaining, or are we other-person centered? Is it always about "me and mine" or is it about "you and yours?" Do we encourage and lift others' spirits, or do we drag them down by whining and complaining (including on social media) about our problems? Do we brighten a room by entering or just by leaving? Too many take the approach that they don't mind suffering silently—as long as the whole world knows about it.

Conversely, in everything we say (directly and indirectly), if we are mature, we project a positive attitude.

Mature folks also *have a plan*. Whether it involves family, friends, career, finances, or personal growth, maturity means that we do not view life as something that just happens to us. We accept the hand we are dealt, and then proceed proactively. We never consider ourselves victims.

Let me illustrate. Some years ago, Sherry and I had the exterior of our home refurbished. We were impressed with what a difference it made in the appearance. We were even more impressed with the person who did the work. Sherry knew him as a teaching colleague. I had never met him, though I now greatly admire him!

Though teaching, by itself, is hard work and far more than a full-time job, this gentleman worked nearly every weekend at our house—for months! Yet, he has ongoing health issues that would have caused many to just sit down and have an endless pity party. Not him. As if he doesn't already have enough to do with teaching, home repair, and his health, he also runs several miles several days a week. He exudes a great attitude and a plan for his life.

Yet, not only do mature folks evidence mature qualities in their speech and proactive lifestyle. They demonstrate maturity in *patience and persistence*. The two go hand in hand.

I find in my own life that when I'm inclined to give up, it's often because I'm impatient for results. That is generally about the same time that I've forgotten two very important facts: (1) The most important reward of any endeavor is not what a person gets as an end result, but what one becomes in the process. Also, what we get is usually proportionate to what we have become. (2) The crop (results) often comes up in places we never planted seed, but if we don't plant somewhere it will come up nowhere. This consistent planting requires the maturity of patience and persistence. Some things we work for; others we wait for. Most often we must work *while* we wait!

Above all, maturity is evidenced in *humility*. C.S. Lewis said: "Humility is not thinking less of yourself but thinking of yourself less." If that's true, and it is, then who else might we think of *besides* ourselves? Mature people already know the obvious answer, as well as the fact that consistently thinking of others is an ongoing challenge. Real grownups know that, as leadership guru John Maxwell says, "The whole world—with one minor exception—is made up of other people."

LEADERSHIP TIP: Grow up to go up!

But grow in the grace and knowledge of our Lord and Savior Jesus Christ.
— 2 Peter 3:18a

A BIT MORE MATURITY

Sherry and I have been blessed with three wonderful children who are now married and have children of their own. They all live in distant places and, though we see them as often as possible, they have lives of their own. Thankfully they are all doing well.

In a recent conversation with a friend, I told him that I believe I do a pretty good job of staying out of our children's business. In that respect, I'm a mature father. I also pointed out that in another area I have a ways to go on the maturity scale. That area has to do with attitude or, more specifically, my happiness as it relates to our children's happiness.

I once read that one of the greatest attitudinal mistakes of parents is the mistaken notion that we can only be as happy as our least happy child. That's not a mature approach.

As we know, everyone has problems and unhappy times. That's life. However, no matter the age of our children, when they are unhappy we tend to internalize it. We don't like for them to hurt in any way. And, often we feel guilty about our own happiness during times when our children are unhappy.

Such feelings make happiness circumstantial, which is always precarious. Whether the circumstances are

19

yours, your children's, or anyone else's, they are constantly changing. Therefore, attitude that is tied to *any* person or set of circumstances, good or bad, is highly unstable. Mature attitudes, on the other hand, don't depend on such variables. They are the result of disciplined, mature thinking, regardless of circumstances.

Speaking of maturity, John Maxwell, said that you "can be young only once, but you can be immature indefinitely." It's far better not to be immature at all. Along this line, we've previously looked at a few signs of maturity. They include positive speech, proactive lives, patience, persistence, and humility. Let's look at several additional signs of maturity as it relates to proper attitudes.

Most definitely, attitude comes into play when two people differ. First of all, it determines *how we view disagreement*. It also has a tremendous impact on how we treat those with whom we disagree.

Film studio executive Darryl F. Zanuck observed: "If two men on the same job agree all the time, then one is useless. If they disagree all the time, then both are useless." Some differences of opinion are good. What better way to learn and grow than by an exchange of ideas? On the other hand, there is no virtue in simply being disagreeable. That is what some wit has described as being in the "objective case and the kickative mood." It's not a sign, as some seem to think, of superior intelligence. It's a sign of immaturity.

It's also immature to view all who disagree with us as enemies. Often those who disagree are trying to help us in some way. Whether they are or not, immaturity is evident when either party in a discussion allows the issue to become bigger than the relationship.

Closely related to how we handle disagreement is the matter of *listening*. Consider that there is no real basis for disagreement until we have listened well enough to the other person to be able to repeat, to his or her satisfaction, what was just said.

Additionally, listening attentively to *everyone* practically shouts maturity. Without butting in, looking around, checking phone messages, or letting the mind wander, the disciplined person pays close attention when others talk.

"That's easier said than done," you say? Indeed! I might also add that some people are easier to listen to than others. This is where our final point on maturity comes in—*acceptance*.

Have you ever considered that perhaps we might be too critical of others? That accepting has often been replaced with rejecting? That we tend to accept only those who are just like us or those who have not inconvenienced us in some way?

Comedian George Carlin illustrated this hypercritical attitude very well. "Have you ever noticed that anybody driving slower than you is an idiot, and anyone going faster than you is a maniac?" In areas besides driving, have we similarly so narrowed the field regarding those we accept, that we feel many do not deserve our full attention?

LEADERSHIP TIP: Grow up to go up.

There is an appointed time for everything. And there is a time for every event under heaven...a time to laugh.
— *Ecclesiastes 3:1, 4*

GROWNUP HUMOR

Those who know anything about me know I love a good story. The funnier the better. I'm constantly listening to others and reading various things to get a good story for use in writing or speaking. However, I've discovered, as perhaps you have, that some things that are supposed to be funny aren't. While the intent might be cleverness or wit, the effect is often one of annoyance or offense.

There is no question that a pun, a good line, or a good story can help us sell ourselves, our ideas, our products, or our services. Humor can also relieve stress, deflect criticism, and build a bridge of communication. In extolling the virtues of humor, Mark Twain said, "Humor is the great thing, the saving thing. The minute it crops up, all our irritations and resentments slip away and a sunny spirit takes their place." But, we must be careful. What we think is humor is not always funny.

Having read this far in the book, you know that I've already said that the first requirement of a joke is that it be funny. Close friends would be quick to say *that* requirement means some of my jokes are in trouble. In casual conversation, I often try out material on them before taking it on the road. (For example, I tell them about the guy who was addicted to brake fluid. He said he could stop anytime.) Some of it is pretty corny and not that funny. So, by their groans, I know not to use certain stuff in presentations.

However, though sometimes corny, the jokes don't hurt my friends. That is definitely not funny. We must always remember that everything said in jest must be free of offense or harm to all present, especially our spouses. Otherwise, it's not good humor. It's a form of meanness, and saying "I was just kidding" does nothing to cover the cruelty.

Humor must also be used in moderation, unless one is performing as a professional comedian. Though I try to use an abundance of humor in my presentations, it can easily be overdone. Then an audience loses sight of the message and leaves with nothing of value—no takeaway.

In serious conversation, few people are more frustrating than those who will not get serious. It causes them to lose credibility, because it is seen as distracting and unprofessional. In this regard, it is also good to bear in mind that in meetings as well as other situations (though humor can temporarily relieve the stress of a problem or can create a positive atmosphere for solving the problem), humor alone will not solve the problem.

In close connection with what we just noticed, permit me to stress that there is a time and a place for humor. When this principle is abused, it's not funny.

I know a gentleman who, no matter where he sees you or the circumstances under which he sees you, he has a joke for you. Without so much as a "Hi, how are you?", he is off and running with some canned something or another that he thinks is funny. I believe you could be running to or from a fire and he would use the same approach. He is oblivious to people and circumstances. Any time is joke time! Though we're glad he is apparently in a good mood, his timing is often irritating. Professional speakers and comedians know that timing in the delivery of a joke is critical. For most of us, timing on *when* to use humor and when not to use it is even more important!

LEADERSHIP TIP: There is no substitute for maturity in communication. When it comes to humor in communication, immaturity is not a laughing matter.

Let all bitterness and wrath and anger and clamor and slander be put away from you, along with all malice.
– Ephesians 4:31

A STORY THAT MUST BE TOLD

It's fall at Terrell Wells Junior High School in San Antonio, Texas. The year is 1963.

President John F. Kennedy is the topic of conversation with students and teachers. He has just left San Antonio on his way to Dallas. Emotions are running high. Those who love him *really* love him. Those who don't—*really* don't.

During home room, students are casually milling around the room, chatting, and waiting to go to afternoon classes. It seems like a good time for informal political discussions. Especially is this a great idea since fourteen- and fifteen-year-olds know just about everything there is to know about politics—and everything else. The discussion heats up so much that one student decides to make his point in a dramatic, though very disrespectful, way. Because he has grown up in an environment where JFK is intensely disliked, he dislikes him. So, with all the confidence and boldness that often goes with ignorance, he makes his move.

At the front of the classroom, high on the wall, hung a nice framed picture of the president. The young student climbs on a chair and, with disdain for the president, dusts an eraser on the picture.

The teacher goes into orbit over what I did. He angrily says I will have to stay after school for such outrageous, disrespectful conduct.

A short time later, that same afternoon, an announcement is made over the school intercom. The president has been shot in Dallas. Later that afternoon, November 22, 1963, we receive another announcement. President John F. Kennedy is dead.

The teacher previously mentioned very quietly walked over to me and compassionately told me I did not have to stay after school. I guess he figured I was already suffering enough for my youthful stupidity.

This sad story is on my mind because at lunch recently our daughter, Amanda, asked if I remembered where I was and what I was doing when Kennedy was shot. I had never told her my story. Because our impressionable little granddaughters were with us in the restaurant and because of the strongly divided political sentiments in our country, I felt it was a story that must be told.

I consider myself a humorist. I tell stories that make relevant points, while making people laugh. However, there is *nothing* funny about the story I just told. But there are important points to be drawn from it.

One point is that good people can be wrongly influenced. I was not a bad kid, and what I did was totally out of character for me. My parents were not bad parents. They were great. We were just prejudiced. Why we were prejudiced is not important. Type of prejudice is.

There is prejudice of the mind, and there is also prejudice of the heart. One involves preferences and things. The other involves people and character.

One type of prejudice can make us annoying in conversation with those who, for instance, like Ford products when we, on the other hand, have a strong bias toward Chevrolet. But it's otherwise harmless. The other type of prejudice *can* create hatred. It's contagious, dangerous, and often destructive. It can easily be taught to children and is often intensified through the reproduction of attitudes. And what's scary is that the process can occur in otherwise good people and families.

The second point of this story relates to something Benjamin Franklin said: "If passion drives you, let reason hold the reins." It's fine to take a position, whether in an election, in the workplace, in society, or in the home. It's fine to feel passionately about something. It's not fine to do or say something that is hateful or destructive or that you might later regret.

LEADERSHIP TIP: There is a fine line between being passionate about something and being bitter toward those who are passionate about something else. Beware of the type of prejudice that carries one over the line.

"God is opposed to the proud, but gives grace to the humble."
— James 4:6b

WHEN WE MESS UP

From the time Sherry and I married nearly forty-eight years ago, we've had a standing agreement. (It's amazing we've been married so long, since I was ten, and she was eight when we married.) Obviously, we had a marriage "agreement," but the agreement that I have in mind involves something that began when we started dating.

This particular agreement goes like this: I will open the car door for you every time we go somewhere together. You will wait until I get around to the other side of the car, and you will not open the door before I can get to it.

We have each, for the most part, held up our end of the agreement. The times I forgot my part, she simply stood there—waiting. After three days, I finally got the message.

I have not told this to make myself sound chivalrous, or to appear like the perfect husband. I'm far from it. I'm rather a work in progress.

I've related the above to lead into some things about mistakes and poor choices. We all make them. When we do, what should we do next?

Suppose that one day, while performing door duty, I got distracted and accidentally slammed Sherry's finger in the car door. Painful? Horrible pain! Would she like it?

Of course not. Nor would I! However, after the pain and shock wore off, she would eventually be okay. *We* would be okay.

Throughout the incident, I would apologize profusely, because I would be sincerely sorry. There would be no *buts* included in the heartfelt expressions of apology. No excuses. Just "I'm so sorry."

Additionally, I would tell her what I plan to do in the future to prevent the same mistake from ever reoccurring. "Sweetheart, in the future I will always check to be sure it is safe to close the door. I promise it won't ever happen again."

In contrast to our illustration, let's call to mind what is often the case, as involves the famous we see on TV—and sometimes with the rest of us. We witness apology after apology, with no specific reference at all to what steps are being taken to avoid making the same mistake again.

Often, there is something else that is lacking. It is the distinction that must be made between a mistake and a choice.

Let's go back to our illustration. If Sherry and I are having a huge argument before I go around the car to open her door, and when she steps out of the car I do the unthinkable and punch her in the face, that is not a mistake. That's a choice. A *very* bad choice!

The steps for resolution are the same—a sincere apology and a future plan. However, in this case there is one more step (in addition to righting things with the Lord) that figures into the process—restoration of trust. That might be a big problem, because whether or not she trusts me in the future would be for her to decide. That would be her decision. I would certainly do my part toward the future and toward rebuilding that trust, but it might not be possible for enough to ever be done to regain her trust.

There are mistakes and there are bad choices. To further illustrate this distinction, we might say that botching a project would be a mistake. Embezzling from the company is a bad choice.

Mistakes are unavoidable. That is why pencils come with erasers. We are human. Mistakes can usually be resolved. Poor choices, on the other hand, are much different and more difficult, if not impossible, to completely resolve.

LEADERSHIP TIP: Know the difference between mistakes and poor choices and the various steps for dealing with each.

For whoever has (used), to him shall be given (more), and he shall have an abundance; but whoever does not have (use), even what he has shall be taken away from him.
— Matthew 13:12 (comments added)

WHAT DID YOU LEARN?

There are those who fly more than I do. I do my share, and on one trip did more than my share.

This stretch of air time began with a flight from San Antonio to Houston, and then from Houston to St. Louis. In the city of the arch, I addressed a national insurance conference before leaving for a conference of European mystery shopping providers in Sardinia, Italy.

The morning that I spoke in St. Louis, I made it a point to go to the hotel registration desk to ask a favor regarding my next day's flights to Italy. Since I would be speaking at the exact time when the airline would begin allowing passengers to print boarding passes, I needed someone to go online to print them for me. The manager at the desk was most accommodative. As per my request he even got me a window seat. That way I could sleep on the nine-hour night flight to Rome without being repeatedly bumped by the serving cart. I was set!

After a wonderful St. Louis conference, I flew to Philadelphia. There I boarded the flight to Rome. From Rome I would fly, in a few days, to Sardinia.

As I approached my assigned seat on the airbus to Rome, I immediately saw a problem. A cute little girl about ten or twelve years old was seated in *my window seat.*

As I pondered the situation, the dad walked up. "Is she in your seat?" he pleasantly asked. First responses are not always best. So, I was glad I exercised a little restraint before answering.

The dad explained that they wanted to sit side by side, but the airline had assigned them seats directly across the aisle from each other. "Would you mind switching with me, and taking the seat across the aisle, so that we can sit together?" he asked. What was I to do? Suddenly my window seat didn't seem all that important.

After a fabulous European conference and while in the airport in Cagliari, Sardinia, prior to my return flight, I related the preceding story to my conference friend, Mike. "So," I bemoaned, "in spite of all my planning I *still* got an aisle seat."

Mike's reply was funny and to the point: "So what did you learn from that?" I would ask each of us the same question regarding all life's experiences. More importantly, I would ask if perhaps we need to rethink our approach to our experiences. To help in that regard, let's consider the following questions.

1. *Do we learn what we should from our experiences?* Mark Twain said that the cat that sits on a hot stove lid won't ever sit on a hot stove lid again. The problem, he noted, is that it also won't ever sit on a cold one. We, too, often learn the wrong lessons from our experiences. When my friend asked what I had learned, I jokingly replied, "Being nice has a price!" Wrong lesson. What I really learned was, "Good manners are made up of petty sacrifices" (Emerson).

2. *Do we merely have experiences or do we gain meaningful experience?* The difference here is determined by three

things: keeping our eyes and minds open, drawing the right lessons from our experiences, and making necessary application. Keep in mind that without application, the lessons are worthless. I might also add that without seeing the *commonality* of experiences to similar situations that arise and without making application of the lessons to these situations as well, we lack true *common* sense.

3. *Do we enrich the lives of others by our experiences?* While I would not suggest that we give unsolicited advice, I would advocate using words to the wise in the form of stories. In relating our experiences in stories, we use *the* most effective form of communication, while fixing the lessons gleaned from our experiences firmly in our minds and those of our listeners. It can also be a subtle, non-threatening way of helping others to avoid our mistakes, while reminding ourselves to be more careful in the future.

LEADERSHIP TIP: Successful leaders are not content until life's experiences become common-sense experience.

And do not be conformed to this world, but be transformed by the renewing of your mind, that you may prove what the will of God is, that which is good and acceptable and perfect.
– Romans 12:2

HOW TO BE BETTER THAN YOURSELF

It happened again this morning. My mouth nearly got me into trouble.

As is my normal Sunday morning routine, I stopped at a convenience store to get Sherry her newspaper. As I approached the door, I noticed a young man who was also making his way to the door. I held the door open, as he walked through—without appearing to notice that I was even there.

Since, of course, I'm the general manager of the universe, I came very close to straightening him out on the proper use of the phrase, "Thank you." But, I decided to take the day off from my GM role.

When we got inside the store, he turned to me and sort of looked me up and down. Then he asked if I was who he thought I was. Yep, that would be me. Whew! I'm glad I had kept my mouth shut at the right time.

Actually, I'm better at that than I used to be. With age has come a little maturity. Sometimes age comes all by itself. However, there was something that happened on a cruise ship many years ago that caused me to mature rather suddenly with respect to controlling my tongue. The incident comes to mind quite often.

After giving my morning enrichment lecture on a Princess ship, I made my way to the business center so that I could check my e-mails. There were several passengers already on the computers. So, I had to wait my turn. That was fine. However, I noticed one fellow who was being very inconsiderate. The more inconsiderate he became, the angrier I became.

Just as I was about to straighten him out in no uncertain terms, another passenger entered the business center. "Mr. Sumerlin," he said. "Good to see you again. I enjoyed your presentation this morning." Suddenly, I decided it would be best if I forgot altogether what I was about to say to the first fellow.

That night I nearly had nightmares regarding the disastrous results had I gotten into a verbal altercation with a passenger over his use of a computer—or over anything else. It would likely have gotten back to the agency I worked for, and that would have been the end of our arrangement. I was so thankful I had held my tongue.

Sometimes the worst thing we can do is just be ourselves. For most of my life, were I to be myself I would verbally give vent to a bad temper. On this, I've worked very hard *not* to be myself. Age has helped with this, because I've mellowed a bit. Also, I've discovered that the long-lasting consequences of expressing negative emotions are not worth the short-lived feelings of power and importance.

The real issue here, though, is not just a matter of consequences. Much of that ultimately involves loss of reputation. What I'm most concerned about is loss of character. That is something altogether different.

Character involves who we really are, regardless of who might see us, hear us, or be involved with us. It means that with respect to true values we are the best that we can be, and that we're trying to be better every day. In that case, reputation will take care of itself.

LEADERSHIP TIP: When tempted to risk reputation by just "being yourself," weigh the situation in the light of character and be better than yourself.

For through the grace given to me I say to every man among you not to think more highly of himself than he ought to think; but to think so as to have sound judgment.
– Romans 12:3

STRENGTHEN STRENGTHS

Today I jogged a couple of miles on the treadmill. I didn't tell you that so that I'd be rewarded with brass bands, lots of attaboys, or even a pat on the back. Nor does working out necessarily make me special.

My motives for working out are not especially noble: I want to live a while longer and I also want something to tell my doctor, during my January physical, that will offset the fact that I quit taking my cholesterol medication. That's not a course of action I necessarily recommend for others, but I really dislike taking medication.

As I was on the treadmill, I was thinking about how jogging is something I can do that doesn't require much athleticism. Then a recent speaking engagement in Odessa, Texas, came to mind as a reminder that I'm not much of an athlete.

After a luncheon and the speech, I participated in a golf tournament. Though I hardly ever play golf, I used to play a lot. Several years ago, I took lessons from a friend who is a club pro. Though he's a great instructor, I'm still not a very good golfer. So, before leaving for the engagement, I decided to go to the driving range several times for practice. It didn't help much. At the tournament, I was still awful. Fortunately, my speech was much better than my golf.

I've never been very talented at any sport. I did try to run track once in junior high. I found out that I had very deceptive speed. I was slower than I looked. But, all that's okay. I've decided to simply do my workout, stay with what I do best, and forget about the rest, unless I want to engage in a certain activity for mere enjoyment.

I've also taken the same approach with other areas of my life in which I don't feel especially strong. For instance, back when I was speaking on cruise ships I always participated in passenger karaoke night. I laugh every time I think of the passenger I met on a shore excursion one day. When he learned I was the enrichment lecturer, his comment was, "I heard you sing at karaoke the other night, and I sure hope you're a better speaker than you are singer." Though once or twice I've been accused of being a great singer, I've always been acquitted for lack of evidence.

On the other hand, though I may be lacking talent in sports, singing, or other areas, there was a time years ago when, if you wanted to get a good haircut, I'd be the guy to go to. In fact, though I haven't barbered professionally in years, I would have no fear of matching barber skills with anyone, anywhere. Additionally, I'm skilled as a speaker and writer. I'll let audiences and readers decide how much skill that might be. But, regardless, barbering, speaking, and writing are all areas of *strength* that I've worked on and have strengthened as a result of intense effort.

As for working on areas of *weakness*, consider this: Because one lacks natural ability or aptitude in the area in which he or she is very weak, there is a significant limit to how much one can improve, regardless of effort. (This has no reference to a character weakness.) In other words,

I'll never be a great golfer or singer no matter what I do. I might raise my skill level in those areas (on a scale of 1 to 10) from a 3 to a 5, provided I work very hard on improvement. But, I would still be mediocre because, in those areas, I lack natural ability. On the other hand, though my interest is no longer in barbering, in the areas of speaking and writing I have unlimited potential for improving my strengths.

Many of us, failing to take proper assessment of our weaknesses as well as our strengths, handicap our self-improvement, and persist in frustration. For that reason, we should often partner with those who are strong where we are weak.

For instance, some years ago, I realized that writing, not editing, is what I do best. So, I accepted the offer of a very talented friend to do my editing for me. Now Paul Smith and I are great friends, and he has made me a more careful writer. I greatly appreciate his unique skills and friendship.

The opportunities for such relationships are many. But they require effective leaders to admit they are weak in certain areas and that they need help.

LEADERSHIP TIP: Strengthening a skill in which we are weak will often result in becoming mediocre and frustrated, while strengthening a strength has the potential for greatness.

Also, do not take seriously all words which are spoken.
— Ecclesiastes 7:21a

A POSITIVE SPIN ON FEEDBACK

I sat down to read the feedback forms from a recent program at which I was the presenter. One immediately got my attention: "It was a total waste of time and money."

I have thought since, *Shucks, if he had just not paid for it, then at the most the guy could only be 50% right.* But that provides little consolation. It still bugs me.

I guess part of the pain comes from the fact that in over twenty-five years as a speaker I have never received more harsh criticism. Also, I know that I worked very hard on that occasion to deliver the best I had. Yet, all that aside, I keep coming back to three questions: What does the comment reveal regarding all feedback? What can we learn from such painful experiences? What would demonstrate Christian leadership?

1. *We must consider our emotional state at the time of the feedback.* A week later, sitting in my office, I felt much different from how I felt when I first read the comment. I'd had time to rest up from the most demanding three weeks of my life, of which the program in question was second to last. Following the presentation, I was bone tired. So, the criticism was viewed from that emotional perspective. General Douglas MacArthur said: "Fatigue makes cowards of us all." So does stress,

insecurity, worry, fear, disappointment, and anxiety. All of these emotions must be taken into account when receiving feedback, because any of them can affect how we receive it.

2. *We must consider the emotional state of the critic.* He (she), too, might be dealing with stress, insecurity, worry, etc. Or, as seems to be the case with the one who gave the harsh criticism, he might have an axe to grind. Though the person apparently needed *everything* in the communication program, as far as I could tell he was not interested in *any* of it. Perhaps he was *volun-told* to be there. Yet, we've all heard that you get out of something what you put into it. For whatever reason, he or someone else put *only* money into it. So, he got nothing out of it. Though we're not trying to judge him or anyone else, we are trying to be objective regarding all feedback. We always want to know, if possible, the reason behind it.

3. *Focus on the content.* If as humorist Will Rogers said, he never met a person he didn't like, then obviously he never met some of the folks that you and I have. Some people are just not very likeable, and these same people are even less likeable when they give feedback. There is no reason a person giving his or her point of view has to be mean-spirited or hateful. But some critics are. In spite of that, we might still benefit from their input. In my case, the strong words motivated me to give the best program of my life the very next day. I fine-tuned a few things, and I'm confident that had my *friend* been present, he would have thought it was at least not a *total* waste of time and money. So, our own

attitude has more to do with the value of criticism than does the attitude of the one giving it.

4. *Keep a good sense of humor.* Mark Twain said: "Against the assault of laughter, nothing can stand." That is why I started this article as I did (in the second paragraph), and then why I sprinkled it throughout with humor. Humor saves the day and makes even the toughest days bearable.

LEADERSHIP TIP: Always make feedback a positive part of growth.

For if anyone thinks he is something when he is nothing, he deceives himself.
– Galatians 6:3

COLD FACTS ABOUT
SELF-IMPORTANCE

We woke up to a very cold, but dry, Sunday morning. We had attended our son's promotion ceremony at Tinker AFB in Midwest City, Oklahoma, the previous afternoon, and I now had a decision to make.

While seated alone in the hotel breakfast area at 5:30, I was watching the weather reports on TV. Heavy snow was on its way.

The decision I referred to was whether to awaken Sherry and our seven-year-old grandson Jackson (who was sleeping over with us) or let them sleep. Whether to call Jon to pick up his son or let Jon sleep. Whether to try to beat the storm and make a run for the Dallas area and home, or stay put in the hotel where we were safe and warm.

Finally, I woke up Sherry, and we made the decision. Within minutes Jon was there to pick up Jackson, our car was packed, breakfast was eaten, and we were on the road. In less than an hour, we knew we were in trouble. Driving conditions had quickly gone from dry to a slight dusting of snow to poor visibility to "Where is the lane I'm supposed to be driving in?"

As we approached the overpasses and bridges, there was the fear of going into a skid on black ice. Worse still was the fear of sliding over the steep embankments at the approaches to the overpasses and bridges.

Then we were gripped by another fear. This resulted from seeing cars that had skidded off the highway and were stuck in deep snow. The next day we even saw eighteen-wheelers that were also stuck in the snow—over on their sides. Having no food, water, or blankets, our fear involved being totally unprepared for very frightful possibilities.

Finally, we decided to get off the highway in the small town of Purcell, Oklahoma. What we found was certainly not like anyplace where meeting planners I know typically book conferences. That was for sure! But, we were greatly relieved and very thankful that the tiny, grungy motel had a vacancy. Five stars were for another time and vastly different circumstances!

It had been an unbelievable morning for folks who had spent most of their lives in south Texas where we rarely saw any snow at all. It was also a learning experience, beginning with a lesson on not ignoring facts.

I thought I had to get home to attend a meeting the next day. Weather channels were telling everyone that the storm was on its way and were advising drivers to stay off the highways.

Though I'm normally an *open-minded* fellow, in this case because of the meeting, I was prejudiced against the weather reports. This should serve to remind us all that whatever the causes for setting aside facts, there are certain prejudices that can have serious consequences.

Another lesson the experience taught me was: When you find yourself in a hole, *stop digging*. Because of poor judgment, I had figuratively driven us into a deep hole.

Fortunately, I had sense enough to stop digging *and* to change plans. I asked Sherry's advice and then followed it. We stopped driving! It was the second time she had given her advice. The first time (before we left Midwest City), prejudice had affected my hearing, and put us in the fix we were in. This time my hearing worked just fine.

When we make bad decisions in life and find ourselves in a hole, remember that not only should we stop digging. We should also recognize that a bad choice is not improved by another bad choice. *Stop digging and start thinking clearly* about what would be a better course of action. What does the Lord want me to do?

Most important of all, I learned that smart folks *recognize two types of misfortune* or tragedy: the type that pursues us and the type that we pursue. Smart folks make the best of the former and avoid the latter.

LEADERSHIP TIP: Listen to your better judgment and to sound words.

Section Two: Communication

Everything we do or say, in every way, every day, throughout the day, intentionally and unintentionally, sends a positive or negative message to others.

But let everyone be quick to hear, slow to speak and slow to wrath.

— James 1:19

HOW TO REALLY LISTEN

"**I** heard that!" Often, we say this when we strongly agree with something that has been said, or when we know something to be true. My question is, "How often do we *really* hear that?" In order for us to *really hear* what is being said, we have to *really listen*. How do we do that?

One requirement for *really listening* is really respecting the person speaking. Showing respect to the speaker can be difficult sometimes. Perhaps you have noticed how much easier it is to listen to some people than to others. There are those whose body language, tone of voice, or word choice is distracting. And then there are those who never seem to get to the point. We've all been in the rather challenging position of trying to listen to someone ramble on endlessly, when the speaker at last attempts to sum up the interminable yarn by saying, "Well, to make a long story short...." You want to scream, "You missed that opportunity an hour ago!"

Aside from the fact that some talkers make it hard for us to be good listeners, leaders nonetheless show respect by listening well to everyone. That doesn't mean everything everyone says is as as valuable as gold, or that we must give everyone our attention forever. But it does mean that they are fellow human beings, and that we can learn something from everyone.

Ralph Waldo Emerson said, "In my walks, every man I meet is my superior in some way, and in that I learn from him." I don't think Emerson was saying that everything others might teach us is correct or that it is to be imitated. From others we might learn what *not* to accept or practice. But we can still learn from them. Knowledge and wisdom come in all forms, but only to those who show respect by *really listening* to others.

Taking this thought a step farther, respect will lead us to be *focused* listeners. Among other things, this means that—without texting, e-mailing, Facebooking or anything else—we give the speaker the greatest compliment of all: our undivided attention. Too often, not understanding is not a hearing issue. It's a focus issue.

Focusing involves eye contact and concentration. It also involves awareness of distractions. In addition to the technological distractions just mentioned, there are also those having to do with environment, prejudices, self-consciousness, stress, or anxiety.

We might also include in this list those thoughts we are preparing to express in response and the urgency we feel to express them. This feeling is a real listening challenge with many. In fact, it has been humorously said that most would not bother listening at all were it not for the expectation and hope that when the other person is through talking it will be their turn to talk. Awareness is necessary before one can successfully eliminate this urgency and all other distractions that can affect our listening focus.

Once we become more aware, we are in a frame of mind to step up our focus by interacting with the one who is speaking. This might involve such actions as leaning in, nodding, rewording various statements, smiling, or interjecting one- or two-word responses of agreement and encouragement. We might also ask questions like why or how, in order to draw ourselves in and the speaker out. These conversational tools help us to forget about ourselves and to focus our attention on the person talking. These tools are the essence of effective listening—and class!

LEADERSHIP TIP: Effective listening starts in the heart and spreads to the eyes and ears.

Therefore be shrewd as serpents, and innocent as doves.
— Matthew 10:16

THE WORST HAIRCUT I'VE EVER SEEN

What I'm about to relate has to be about the strangest thing I've ever witnessed. It happened in the days when I owned an old-fashioned barbershop in Alamo Heights, a suburb of San Antonio.

It was a quiet Friday morning when in walked a lady with her blond-haired, teenage son. They had been coming in for years. So, we greeted one another warmly.

"Can you fix this haircut?" she asked.

"Sure," I replied. "He didn't get this here, did he?"

"Yes," she answered. "We were in yesterday afternoon."

Since I only worked in the mornings and Lisa worked in the afternoons, it wasn't hard for me to figure out who the boy's barber was.

"Lisa did this?" I asked incredulously.

"Yes, she did," she quickly replied.

I was stunned! Lisa had been with me for years and is a good barber. And, even if she weren't, a blind barber in his first day of barber school wouldn't have cut a head of hair to look like that. I'd never seen anything like it—deep gouges and just hacked up!

I apologized profusely to the lady and said I would talk to Lisa about it. In the meantime, she and her son wanted me to just fix the haircut without cutting it any shorter.

Though there wasn't much I could do under the circumstances and with their restrictions regarding shortening it, I did the best I could and told them they didn't owe me for the repair. Again, I apologized, and they left.

Two hours then remained before Lisa was due to arrive for work. I was in a quandary. What do I tell her? How can I explain how *bad* the haircut was? Will she even understand what I'm talking about? What will she say to explain it? I was terribly bothered by it all.

After a couple of hours, two cars showed up. One was Lisa's. The other belonged to the lady and her son. The shop was empty, thankfully.

Lisa, the mother, and boy arrived at the door at the same time, and through the closed door I could see them talking animatedly. As they came in, the conversation became more heated with each affirming the other to be wrong.

Lisa, a very mild-mannered person, insisted that though she had cut his hair she had *not* cut it like that. The boy and mom insisted she had. I tried to keep things calm, and Lisa immediately went in the office and stayed there.

The boy and mom had returned to request that I go ahead and cut the hair as short as I needed to. Just work out all the bad spots. I did, and that was that.

When they left, and Lisa came out of the office, she still was fuming and insisting she had *not* cut the hair like that. She said that the mom and boy had seriously disagreed over how he wanted his hair cut, but that she gave him a nice haircut that they both seemed to approve of.

"Lisa," I said. "I know you didn't cut that boy's hair like that. You never cut a head of hair like that in your life. I believe you."

We both sort of laughed it off, and agreed something strange was going on at home. But, for certain, Lisa was not responsible for his haircut.

The next day, we were working together when in walked the same folks. The boy was crying and had a note for both of us, and money for the repair I had done. The night before, he had fessed up to his mom. He, in anger and frustration, had butchered his own hair. The mystery was solved.

The obvious lesson from the story would seem to be concerning honesty and the need to for children to learn the value of being truthful at an early age. Courage to admit and correct a wrong would also be a valuable lesson from the story. For learning these lessons the boy is to be commended.

From a leadership point of view, though, permit me to suggest an additional lesson or principle.

LEADERSHIP TIP: Get the story, the whole story, before believing the worst about anyone.

So also you, unless you utter by the tongue speech that is clear, how will it be known what is spoken? For you will be speaking into the air.
— 1 Corinthians 14:9

OUR COMMUNICATION VEHICLE

"Words are vehicles upon which thoughts travel." Audiences have heard me say that for years. I've been unable to find the original source of the quote. So, I have sort of made it my own.

The words conjure up, in my mind, a vivid image. Let's see if they do the same for you.

Think with me, if you will, of your dream car. For some, it might be the car they now drive. For others, ownership of a certain dream car might be just that—a dream. Regardless of whether you now own it or would like to, get a clear picture of that car in your mind.

Now let's transfer that picture to a type of vehicle that provides transportation for thoughts. For that, would we want a clunker or a dream vehicle? Keep in mind that the automobile we drive every day can only get us from point A to point B. A vehicle of thought, on the other hand, can take us to fulfilling business and personal relationships, as well as to positions of influence. Those things being true, what might a dream *vehicle of thought* look like? Using the letters of the word *car* as an acronym, let's build our ideal vehicle of thought.

First of all, let the *c* in car stand for clarity. Mark Twain said: "The difference between the almost right word and the right word is really a large matter—it's the difference between the lightning bug and the lightning." It's also the difference, many times, between being understood and being misunderstood.

Along this line, I'm reminded of the story about the first sergeant who told his new recruits: "I want you to put on a clean pair of socks every day." One young recruit, not understanding that he had to take his dirty socks off first, discovered at the end of the first week that he couldn't get his boots on. Some folks require more clarity in communication than others, but basic clarity must be standard equipment on all communication vehicles.

It must also be equipped with the ask-for-feedback package. Thus, the letter *a* stands for ask.

As a writer, I know that I do not always choose the right vehicle for my thoughts. So, I have a wonderful editor who gives me feedback on everything I write. Sometimes I'm surprised when he tells me what a certain phrase conveys to him. It's not what I had in mind at all.

For all of us, whether we're writing or speaking, it helps to ask others if we're being clear. More specifically, before we take part in an important meeting or conversation we should ask our spouse, friend, co-worker, supervisor, or anyone whose opinion we value if what we plan to say is clear and proper. Also, when we are face-to-face in conversation and the other person has a puzzled look on his or her face, we should politely ask, "What is your understanding of what I just said?" Most importantly, we need to habitually ask ourselves before speaking: "Is what I'm about to say clear and is it going to come out as intended?"

Not only should clarity and asking for feedback be part of the standard equipment of our communication vehicle.

It should also be equipped with responsibility. The *r* in car should serve to remind us of that.

Of all the things our society needs, a sense of responsibility would have to be at the top of the list. Many don't want to be responsible for much of anything.

As an illustration, we've all heard folks say that they are self-made. Of course, when such a claim is made it is always with reference to success—"self-made success." Have you ever heard anyone claim to be a self-made failure? No one wants to accept responsibility for that.

Similarly, few want to accept responsibility for communication failure. Yet, it too is "self-made." How could it be otherwise? (There are certain exceptions involving the other person.) If I'm the one talking, I'm the only one who could possibly be responsible for what comes out of my mouth. Knowing such, and consistently applying that knowledge, should keep my C-A-R from crashing. And when it does crash, I'm generally the one who is liable.

LEADERSHIP TIP: Always keep your vehicle of thought well maintained and all its equipment in proper working order.

Who winks with his eyes, who signals with his feet,
who points with his fingers.
– Proverbs 6:13

WHAT WE MUST KNOW ABOUT
BODY LANGUAGE

A young lady dressed in business attire enters a restaurant. Waiting to be seated, she leans slightly on the hostess stand as if it's been a long day. When she's seated, as per her request, it's at a table as far away from the other guests as possible. She orders, eats her dinner, and reads—without saying anything to anyone but her server. Well, that's not exactly true. To anyone who notices, though not verbally, she says a great deal. She's not rude. However, through body language, she says: "I'm tired. This is my down time and I want to be left alone to eat, read, and unwind."

This illustrates the first thing most of us need to know about body language. Every time we are in the presence of others, we are communicating by this very quiet method. It is unavoidable.

We tend to think that the easiest way to avoid saying the wrong thing is to just say nothing. There are times for all of us when that would certainly be an improvement! However, the *best* way to really avoid sending the wrong message is to always be conscious of what we say *and* do. Facial expressions, gestures, and posture send a message apart from anything we might or might not verbalize.

This leads us to the second thing we need be aware of regarding body language. It can be, and often is, more powerful than words. In fact, when our words and body language convey conflicting messages, guess which message is received?

To answer that question, call to mind something you might have observed at a meeting or conference. The speaker tells you from the podium that he is excited to be your speaker. Yet, there's no smile, no eye contact, and no gestures. The speaker appears far from relaxed. Do you believe that he is excited? After all, that's what he said. But his actions say something different. His actions say that he lacks confidence or that he is scared to death.

Let's transfer that concept to communication both in and out of the workplace. It's a nice thing to tell friends, employees, and customers that you appreciate them. However, they are more likely to believe your words if they see the smile on your face, the acceptance in your eyes, and the warmth in your posture.

This conflict between body language and words, and the power of the former over the later, is something that has been observed by animal trainers. They say that oftentimes the main reason some amateur trainers have little success in training pets is because the animal is confused by conflicting messages. The voice says one thing and the body language says something else. The animal instinctively ignores the words and obeys the body language. People often do the same thing. For that reason, we need to be sure that our body language always matches our verbal communication. If they don't match, our words are going to lose the battle between the two—every time.

The third thing we need to keep in mind is that since communication is a two-way street, we must always be monitoring the other person's body language as well as our own. For instance, if the other person tilts the head, it might mean he/she doesn't understand or doesn't agree. If she looks at her watch, it might mean she is pressed for time. In that case, now might not be a good time to talk. For effective communication, we must listen *and* look for what is said, and then we must adapt accordingly.

Finally, we must not to jump to hasty, erroneous conclusions regarding the actions or mannerisms of others. Body language is best assessed contextually and as a total package, rather than when isolated.

By itself, the fact that the arms are crossed may not mean anything other than that the room is cold. It doesn't always mean a person is unapproachable or defensive. It might, but it also might not. Similarly, one might wink because of a nervous tic rather than because he's flirting. During a program one might raise her hand to straighten her hair, rather than to ask the speaker a question. Common sense is always important to accurately determine what message someone is sending.

LEADERSHIP TIP: We are always communicating by what we say as well as by what we do. To communicate effectively, always be conscious of the message we and others are sending, whether by words, actions, or both.

For the dream comes through much effort, and the voice of a fool through many words.
— Ecclesiastes 5:3

HAVE TO VERSUS WANT TO

One day a friend and I were commiserating about occasional writer's block. He was a longtime staff writer for the *San Antonio Express-News*.

He said that quite often he would ask his wife to listen while he read something to her that he had written for the newspaper. However, before he could start reading she would ask, "Is this something you wanted to write or something you had to write?" We both could identify with that. In one case the article would be written because of obligation and a deadline. In the other it would be the result of emotion, conviction, or intense interest.

Though we might not all be writers, we all experience times when, for a variety of reasons, we feel like we *have to* say (not necessarily write) something. It might be because we are asked a direct question or because we are asked for a favor or because we are asking ourselves how we might best impress someone. These are often occasions when right after we have said something—we regret it. So, let's explore what our options are in these situations.

There are times when all of us are asked questions that place us in awkward situations. But, we feel we must say something. This dilemma could be compared to when we take a mouthful of hot coffee. Whatever we feel we have to do or say next is likely to be wrong.

Put another way, these questions put one in a position of having to make a quick, and often, bad decision. Right away we start asking ourselves certain questions. Should I repeat something I shouldn't tell about another person? Should I divulge damaging or confidential information? What will the inquirer think if I don't answer the question or if I'm evasive? Will my answer mean I'm taking sides? Will my answer damage my relationship with the person asking the question or with someone else? We've all been there. So, like the mouthful of hot coffee, we spit out something because we thought we had to.

However, the moment we feel we *have to* say something is the time to stop and think: What might be the *best* thing to say? What are our options?

One approach might be to just say, "I'm sorry, I'm not at liberty to answer that." Another might be, "I'm not comfortable discussing (answering) that." This often implies matters of conscience. Reasonable people are not usually willing to run roughshod over someone else's conscience. So, the I'm-not-comfortable approach is effective in dealing with many types of difficult questions and situations.

Another time when we often feel like we must say something is when someone wants a favor that demands our time. One of the greatest time management tools known to man is the two-letter word: NO. Of course, that's assuming the person doesn't have time for whatever is asked of him or her and would rather not do it.

In such circumstances, why don't we say "no" more often than we do? Often it is because "yes" is reactionary and spoken out of fear of upsetting or hurting the one making the request. We're often thinking that if we make that person unhappy by rejecting their request, then their unhappiness will make us unhappy. The reality is that this is a misguided form of happiness, based on the fickle happiness of another. Also, if in fact we commit to something we don't want to do, just to keep the other person happy so that we can also be happy, we will nonetheless still be unhappy. The cause, overcommitment, will be different, but the feeling of unhappiness will be the same.

What might we say to such requests from a perspective of *want to* rather than have to? We might cushion a "no" statement with such words as "unfortunately." We might also provide validation for why we refused the request or an alternative response such as a future time for when we might be able to commit.

Another dangerous time for feeling we have to say something is when we want to impress others. This might take the form of expressing an aren't-I-smart opinion, or it might take the form of sarcasm. Both are for the purpose of impressing others with our self-importance.

The advantage of one over the other is that if sarcasm fails or is offensive, one can always say, "I was just joking." Obnoxious people are usually clueless in regard to what I'm about to say. The considerate are not. The first requirement of a good joke is that it be funny—to everyone.

The best way to impress is to not make impressing others a goal of communication. That way we talk only when we have something of value to say. If it happens that what we say is in line with the other person's interests, that is *really* impressive.

LEADERSHIP TIP: Be careful about feeling you must say something.

For lack of wood the fire goes out, and where there is no whisperer, contention quiets down.
— Proverbs 28:20

WHEN NOT TO TALK

I was asked if so-and-so is still alive. When I answered "yes" for the millionth time, the response was the same—for the millionth time: "Well, I'm surprised one of his ex-wives hasn't killed him by now." The fact that the fellow's daughter happens to be one of the exes might have biased him and stirred his emotions, just a tad. However, I wondered why we must go through the same song and dance every time he sees me.

I'd had enough! First, I don't care how many ex-wives my acquaintance has, nor is it any of my business. Also, and more important, I feel it is just as bad to listen to gossip as it is to tell it. So, I decided to put a stop to it with a simple suggestion: "Why don't you give him a call and take that up with him?" It suddenly got very quiet.

We would all grant that gossip is not acceptable conduct for a Christian. Let's also consider some practical matters regarding the impact such talk has on character, organizational morale, and relationships.

Although, as we all know, you and I would never engage in this destructive form of speech, perhaps some gentle kick-on-the-shin reminders about gossip would be in order. Keep in mind, though, what Ronald B. Zeh said years ago: "The gossip of the future may not be a backbiting, nosy, tongue-wagging two-face, but a super-megabyte, random-access, digital interface." Gossip can be spoken or written.

The first thing we need to remember is what this form of speech says about one's character. Though we will grant that sometimes what we say about others is not as much a matter of character as it is carelessness, we need to give more thought to what we are about to say and then sometimes just not say it. It's so easy to drift from simple, innocent, harmless conversation about others into that which is harmful and should not be repeated, even if it's true. Some folks just talk too much, and should be more careful about what they say.

On the other hand, deliberately telling or repeating that which we know to be harmful to another's reputation strongly suggests a character problem. This, by the way, is vastly different from saying what must be said about someone, saying it to the right person and saying it for the right reasons. That's responsible action, and requires courage. The other is irresponsible, abusive, and cowardly.

Another thing about gossip is what it does to the reputation of the one who makes it a habit. It makes that person someone who can't be trusted. It tells others that anything said to him or her, even in confidence, is not secure. It also says that if that person will gossip to you, the same person will gossip *about* you. As a result, trusting a gossip becomes a huge issue in relationships and business.

Gossip also indicates a lack of emotional and/or intellectual maturity. Those who are comfortable and secure with themselves don't feel the need to tell things about others in an attempt to tear them down. Rather, they are inclined to say things that build them up. In this respect, they're genuine leaders!

With regard to maturity and how it impacts what we talk about, it might be good for everyone to keep in mind what Socrates said: "Strong minds discuss ideas, average minds discuss events, weak minds discuss people."

Finally, slander can come back to bite us. What makes its way to our ears, and then is repeated by us, can just as easily make its way to the ears of those who will take action.

Notice that for the first time I used the word *slander* in place of *gossip*. It has legal connotations. Slander that we have spoken and is then repeated back to us could be very embarrassing. It could be worse than embarrassing when repeated back to us in court.

LEADERSHIP TIP: Before speaking, carefully consider the what, the how, the why, the of whom, and the to whom.

A time to be silent, and a time to speak.
— Ecclesiastes 3:7b

WHAT IS SAID THROUGH SILENCE

I t's five in the morning at sea on the Sun Princess. I'm alone and all is quiet. My book is open on the table, and coffee is within easy reach. In the huge dining area called the Horizon Court, a few other early birds are seated away from my private area in the far corner. Thus situated, I read, think, write, and wait for my very favorite time on a cruise ship. Sunrise at sea!

In my early speaking years, in the 1990s and 2000s, as an enrichment lecturer for Princess Cruise Lines, I experienced such a quiet, peaceful setting many times. In those days, the average age of the Princess passenger was deceased. So, quietude was not hard to find and was always a treat.

Today I still savor quietude. It's just not always as easy to find. Nowadays even a moment of silence seems to require background music.

When not on the road, my best spot for silence is the travel room of our home, early in the morning. There, surrounded by souvenir plates on the wall overhead and rare books in the glass fronted cabinet, pleasant thoughts often fill my head. Finding comparable retreats elsewhere can be a real challenge.

Author and speaker Fran Lebowitz said: "If thine enemy offend thee, give his child a drum." Obviously, no one cares for that type of noise. On the other hand, we have become a noisy society that seems to abhor silence.

Yet, silence can be priceless! For a leader, it can provide a proper environment for thought, reflection, and meditation. More importantly, *in conversation* it can be more eloquent than words.

There are many times when silence eloquently says we are wise. Let's face it. Most of us talk too much. That being the case, we can easily become like the fellow of whom the witty Sydney Smith said: "He had occasional flashes of silence that made his conversation perfectly delightful."

While maturity involves lots of things, one characteristic is the realization that not everyone needs or wants the benefit of all our opinions and *wisdom*. A mature person also realizes that a person of many words is more apt to not only say nothing, but also to say the wrong thing. Sometimes the only thing required to appear wise is to think of something really dumb to say, and then just not say it.

In addition to what silence says about our wisdom, silence can also say that we are human, and that words fail us. Shakespeare said: "Silence is the perfectest herald of joy; I were but little happy, if I could say how much." In other words, great joy left him lost for words.

Have you ever been that happy? On the other hand, have you ever been so heartbroken, shocked, disappointed, or discouraged that words failed you? It's okay that words failed. In fact, it's better than okay. It tells others that we are people of depth and emotion, that we care, and that we have feelings. Silence on such occasions can be a powerful way of assuring others that we share a common humanness. Then, when the time comes for us to speak, those same folks are more apt to listen.

With respect to listening, silence often says we are considerate and are, in fact, listening to others. While attending an association meeting in Austin, Texas, some years ago, I was reminded of just how powerful an impact silent listening can have.

When I entered the meeting room that morning and greeted the speaker, he immediately said, "Oh, I saw you in the coffee shop a while ago." Then he added, "You're the fellow who asked the lady behind the counter how she was doing, and you actually looked at her like you cared about her answer."

It surprised me that someone had even noticed. It also caused me to think seriously about how lightly we might say things to others or ask questions of them, when we really don't care enough to listen to their response.

Undivided attention is the highest form of appreciation and respect. Conversely, those who cannot be silent in conversation show that they are not very wise, not very approachable, and not very respectful. But they are very self-centered. In fact, if you will just let them finish talking about themselves, they will gladly be quiet so that you can talk about them.

LEADERSHIP TIP: When it comes to silence versus self-interest, choose the high road.

Section Three: Stress

There are two types of stress. One we pursue. The other pursues us.

For this reason I say unto you, do not be anxious.
But seek first His kingdom and His righteousness;
and all these things shall be added to you.
– Matthew 6:25a,33

HOW TO DEAL WITH WORRY

Do you ever worry? I've had people tell me that they never worry about anything. I'll take their word for that. However, for the rest of us, worry can be a problem. It can be a problem for Christians.

We tend to worry about similar things, such as health, careers, family, money, relationships, and cars. Yes, I said cars!

Right now, as I sit in the Catalyst, the coffee shop for the historic General Morgan Inn in beautiful Greeneville, Tennessee, I'm worried about my car. I know, worry can cause insomnia, high blood pressure, and hair loss. (I think I'm in the clear on one of those side effects!) But when I see the "check engine" light on a car with less than 30,000 miles, I worry.

The light has gone on and off for the past 2,500 miles, from Lavon, Texas, to Gettysburg, Pennsylvania, to Washington, D.C., to Greeneville, Tennessee. I've had it checked twice, and I've had the sensor replaced once. On our long anticipated once-in-a-lifetime road trip, the light has been the proverbial fly in the ointment.

But, alas, some good has come from this pesky fly: I get to reflect on how I've dealt with my worry, and I get to share my findings with you.

Many years ago, when Al Smith was governor of New York, he had a way of dealing with worrisome issues. He would say, "Let's examine the facts." That's what I've tried to do regarding my car.

Fact: I've been assured *twice* that we will make it home, with no damage to the engine. Fact: I'm told that only when the light is blinking is there a serious problem, and it has never blinked. Fact: we've made it this far.

Imagination, on the other hand, says the light is going to start blinking, and the car is going to blow up immediately. We will be left standing by the side of some lonely stretch of highway in the middle of the night, waiting to hitch a ride with a serial killer.

Truly, the most powerful nation in the world is imagi-*nation*. So, the first thing I would share on dealing with worry is to silence the imagination and to just deal with the facts. I would even suggest that, as I'm doing now, we write these facts down. This step greatly serves to rein in a wild imagination.

Another thing that has helped me in dealing with the emotional state known as worry is activity. Sherry and I have been so busy having so much fun that the light is often forgotten. A light on the dash of our car meant nothing while we were busy viewing the Washington Monument, Mount Vernon, Monticello, and Montpelier. Time to worry is time to do something worthwhile.

Perspective can also pull you out of a state of worry. The engine light and car mean nothing at all compared to the sacrifices that are represented by Gettysburg or the Lincoln Memorial. In fact, by making such a big deal of such relative trifles, I feel a bit ashamed.

We have so much to enjoy in this life and so much for which to be thankful. Most of what we worry about doesn't ever happen anyway. Let's make it Job #1 to enjoy all the relationships and good things that *do* happen.

LEADERSHIP TIP: Eliminate most worry by grabbing hold of the real moment and letting go of the remote possibility of the worrisome maybes.

The end of a matter is better than its beginning.
Patience of spirit is better than haughtiness of spirit.
— Ecclesiastes 7:8

PROBLEM SOLVING #225

This can't be happening. I swipe my hotel keycard, and the light on the door handle flashes orange instead of green. It's not that unusual in hotels. But it keeps doing it!

I double-check the room number. It's room #225, the same room I was in last night. I have been careful not to put the card near anything that might foul up the code. So, I frantically try again—and again!

Suddenly, without the light turning green, the door opens. What just happened? This *is* my room. I left my stuff in there. Who is this very surprised lady, on the other side of the door, who is trying to figure out why I'm trying to open the door? Where is my stuff? Momentarily, neither of us knows what to say.

Finally, I explain that this is *my* room. I stayed last night, and this is supposed to be my second night in #225. "I'm so sorry," she says. She also says, as I foolishly peer past the open door looking for my things, "Nothing was in the room when I checked in. I feel just awful about the confusion."

Still reeling, and feeling like I'm in *The Twilight Zone*, I head for the elevator and the registration desk. No reservation was made for me for a second night!

Regardless of whether the fault is with my wonderful client or the hotel, the room was not booked. That is clear. But now I have two major concerns: finding my clothes and personal items that were left in the room and getting a room for the night. What if the hotel is completely booked?

Fortunately, the hotel has a room, and housekeeping has my stuff—wadded up in a plastic bag. The client and the hotel are very accommodative. All is fine at last. I'm not sleepless in Phoenix. But here is what I am—a little wiser.

Wisdom says that a problem is not the same thing as a fact, and that it is futile to try to solve a fact. It was a fact that someone else occupied my room. It was also a fact that her stuff was in the room, and my things were somewhere else. Nothing I could do or say was going to put me or my things back in that room. Those were facts!

On the other hand, I had a couple of problems that required solutions. I needed to locate my things—and a room for the night. Housekeeping, the hotel, and my client handled all those issues. The problems were solved.

A large part of the problem-solving process, though, was the result of cool heads. All parties, including the lady who was given my room, remained calm and refrained from blaming the other party. Blame seldom, if ever, solves problems.

Additionally, they were all very sorry for my inconvenience, and they expressed their regret. Though such expressions didn't solve the immediate issues, they did have a calming effect on the only party who needed his blood pressure to return to normal.

Those involved in this unfortunate incident and in fixing the problems provide timely reminders in basic problem-solving technique. We would do well to keep them in mind.

LEADERSHIP TIP: When it is determined that there is a problem and not a fact, remain calm, avoid fixing blame, and empathetically go to work to find an acceptable solution.

Be anxious for nothing, but in everything by prayer and supplication with thanksgiving let your requests be made known to God. And the peace of God, which surpasses all comprehension, shall guard your hearts and your minds in Christ Jesus.
– Philippians 4:6-7

BOILS VERSUS EXECUTIONS

After leaving the house to begin the day, I called my wife and wished her a good day. I could tell by the sound of her voice when she answered the phone that the day was going to be a challenge for her. As a high school math teacher, some days were more challenging than others. I guess that's true for everyone.

Put another way, some days are just easier than others. A lot depends on how we feel—our ever-changing moods, time or people pressures, situations, or perhaps the monotony/tedium of endless tasks. The difficulty is generally not caused by anything that's life-threatening. It's just life from day to day.

That reminds me of an account in Samuel Pepys' *Diary*. He tells of witnessing the execution of Sir Harry Vane in London. He was beheaded, which seems like a rather serious way to die.

According to Pepys, as Sir Harry mounted the platform, he was pleading with the executioner. For his life? Oh no. He was pleading with the executioner to be careful so that when the blade came down it would not strike the painful boil on the back of his neck!

Sir Harry illustrates what is true for most people. We can deal with the executions. Life's boils are another matter.

Sherry is tough. In what was, at the time, her sixteen-year teaching career (she has since retired), she effectively dealt with an execution or two. Perhaps you have dealt with some as well. The question is how can we better handle the daily boils that tend to get us down?

In her book, *Unleashing the Power of Rubber Bands*, Nancy Ortberg says, "Your best leadership efforts are needed on a daily basis right where we are." Great words! But what about those days when we would rather be somewhere else?

One way to deal with such days is to see issues for what they are. They are just a part of life. Wishing life were otherwise won't make it so.

That is not to say that bothersome matters in the course of a day are unimportant. They are very important to the person having to deal with them. However, they must be kept in perspective. As I've said, they are not usually life-threatening.

Along this line, I once read of a corporate president who had a unique way of dealing with issues that were brought to him during the workday. After listening patiently to whoever was telling him all that went wrong, he would always respond, "Well, did anyone die as a result of this crisis?" He would then say that if the problem wasn't serious enough that it resulted in someone's death, it was certainly manageable.

Another bit of wisdom I find useful for day-to-day issues is: "This too shall pass." Now that I'm middle-aged (that's always five years from where we are), I can say from experience that I've found that statement to be true. What we worry about and stress over today is often forgotten tomorrow.

An additional way I have of dealing with day-to-day challenges involves a photograph that I have from the days when I lectured at sea. The picture is of a gorgeous sunrise over the ocean. It serves to remind me that each sunrise brings hope. If the sun rises and I'm part of a new day—there is hope that things will eventually get better.

LEADERSHIP TIP: Leadership is more evident in how we deal with the boils of today than with the executions of tomorrow.

I know how to get along with humble means, and I also know how to live in prosperity.
– Philippians 4:12a

FIVE COMMON-SENSE PRINCIPLES OF MONEY MANAGEMENT

Many years ago, while struggling in business ventures, I had to work out payment arrangements with the IRS. As you might guess, it was not a high point in my life. I was fortunate, though, to have an agent who was almost friendly. In fact, I consider it a badge of honor that as our discussions progressed, her attitude toward me greatly improved. Perhaps she came to understand I was not a deadbeat.

At one point in our contact, I commented that I truly appreciated her patience and understanding. I told her I wanted to send her one of my books in appreciation. I will never forget her response: "I sure hope it's not on money management!" We both laughed.

That was a long time ago. And though I'm not by any means an expert on handling money, through the school of hard knocks I've learned a few common-sense principles. If you already know these things, perhaps it won't hurt to be reminded.

1. We are not our bank balance. When struggling financially, that is very difficult to remember. The reason for this difficulty, it seems, is due to the widely accepted

and erroneous idea that success is determined by our bank balance. If we have a large one, we're successful, and if we don't, we're failures. Unfortunately, this thinking doesn't take into account the godliness, relationships, and accomplishments of the individual, whether wealthy or broke. It also ignores the fact that broke can be a temporary condition, while poor is often a fixed attitude.

2. We seldom have as much money as we think we do. Of all the mistaken notions that got me into financial trouble years ago, this was the biggest. It was often not even with respect to what I had. It was the false notion of what I was going to have—the next big speech, the next book, some sort of windfall. Not only does this lead a person to spend money he doesn't yet possess, it creates a huge problem when one *never* gets the money that was expected.

3. Long-term regret is the price paid for instant gratification. Smarter people than I can talk about interest rates and the monetary cost of a borrowed lifestyle. I, on the other hand, have been to school on the stress it creates. I know about that, and I also know about the joy of paying as you go. There is absolutely no comparison! It's tainted pleasure to have what you can't afford. It results in a painful, stressful loss of peace of mind and self-worth. P.T. Barnum said, "Debt robs a man of his self-respect, and makes him almost despise himself."

4. It's not what you earn, but what you keep. We've all heard, "Pay yourself first." Consumer debt says most are not listening. Not having any sort of savings or emergency fund, many people find that borrowing be-

100

comes a *necessity*. Rarely is doing without in order to save viewed as a necessity. Once again, P.T. Barnum said, "There is more satisfaction in rational saving than in irrational spending." I might also add—there is more self-respect.

5. "It is more blessed to give than to receive." Jesus said that about 2,000 years ago, and, of course, it is still true. Money management is not simply about earning, spending, keeping, and saving. In fact, even when I say "Pay yourself first," giving is not preempted. Rational saving actually positions one to be more generous with others. It also positions a leader (a person of positive influence) to make a greater difference, while living a more abundant life.

LEADERSHIP TIP: Money can be the best of servants and the worst of masters.

So, what is the advantage of him who toils for the wind?
— Ecclesiastes 5:16

REALLY EXPENSIVE WHISTLES

When Benjamin Franklin was seven years old, he decided he just had to have a certain whistle. So, without even asking the price he walked into the toy store, placed all his coppers on the counter and excitedly walked out with his new whistle.

His joy was unbounded as he went all over the house blowing on his new toy. But, it was short-lived joy when his older brothers and sisters found out what he had paid for the whistle and began to make fun of him. Then he came to realize what he had occasion to observe many times in life: we often pay too much for our whistles.

What we perceive as the value of something is often way out of proportion to the cost in time, money, relationships, anxiety, or energy. What we're left with is often disappointment and regret.

My most vivid memory of paying too much for my whistle came in the form of my dream car—a Corvette. I'd long considered how cool it would be to own one. And, of course, the whole world would think I was cool just for driving one.

Finally, the opportunity presented itself. It was many years ago, and I was speaking in Poteau, Oklahoma. What good fortune that there would be someone at the meeting who wanted to sell his white, 1974 Corvette. What a deal!

My banker friend back home was happy to put the deal through. So, instead of taking a return flight home I drove my new car. The first time I stopped to gas up and the lady behind the counter said, "Nice car," I knew I'd made a *great* deal.

Thus began my entrepreneurial venture of flipping (selling) Corvettes. It seemed like such a perfect plan. Problem was my finances at the time were such that if it took 50 cents to go around the world I couldn't have gotten out of sight. But, that didn't matter. With the confidence that goes with ignorance, I initiated a plan to drive the fine sports cars for a while on borrowed money and sell them at a profit. I could have my cake and eat it too.

Aside from the fact I didn't know a thing about cars and knew even less about buying and selling them, another major flaw in my plan developed. I fell in love with my third purchase—a beautiful, yellow, 20,000-mile, 1966 Corvette Stingray. My love affair with this fiberglass beauty went on way beyond the predetermined time, during a period when I definitely couldn't afford it.

Did I enjoy the Stingray? Oh, yes! Were all the admiring looks at traffic lights and the "wows" from friends worth the tremendous financial stress? Not hardly.

Looking back, I know I had a great time in all three Corvettes. However, I jokingly tell friends there is a lot of money to be made in flipping Corvettes—because I *left* a lot of money there for someone else! For me, they were very costly whistles.

The Franklin story, as I recently indicated in conversation with a friend, has many applications. Whether it's better gadgets, nicer automobiles, bigger homes, greater lifestyles, more degrees, dream vacations, rungs on the career ladder, or merely more stuff—what does it cost? Really cost?

The answer often involves more than just money, though that can certainly be an important consideration. It also involves asking the right questions. How much of my life will this actually require? What is the family/relational sacrifice? What is the stress factor, and for how long? What is the health risk? What's the long-term value (objective), and is it worth the trade-offs?

These questions are not asked to be judgmental. Nor can I answer them for you, any more than you can answer them for me. I'm merely concerned that in failing to ask and properly answer the right questions, we wind up swapping things of real value for trinkets and more stuff.

LEADERSHIP TIP: Beware of the type of leadership that knows the price of everything and the value of nothing.

And I have seen that nothing is better than that a man should be happy in his activities, for that is his lot.
— Ecclesiastes 3:22a

CHASING THE UNCATCHABLE

One of the most famous phrases of the United States Declaration of Independence is "life, liberty, and the pursuit of happiness." I'm not totally convinced that, with such a phrase, our founding fathers did us any favors. Many have misunderstood the happiness part.

It seems many of us are about to run ourselves to death in pursuit of happiness. From entertainment to travel to food to thrills to what we own to what we consume, many run faster and faster chasing after happiness and have become unhappier and more frustrated in the process. Perhaps Harriet Beecher Stowe was right when, in *Oldtown Folks*, she said: "People feel the need of amusements less and less, precisely in proportion as they have solid reasons for being happy." Unfortunately, through misconceptions regarding happiness, many have never found those reasons.

Like the fleeting butterfly to a child, happiness seems just beyond our grasp. Could it be that happiness is not a thing, a situation, or a place, but rather a state of mind resulting from purpose and fulfillment?

The pursuit thing can cause us to lose our perspective in life regarding things that really matter, and thus, can leave us feeling empty and unhappy. Other erroneous thought patterns can do the same thing.

Before we look at a few of these misconceptions, permit me to say a word regarding how happiness relates to leadership and team building. Generally speaking, a good attitude broadens and enhances such areas of influence. Though Abraham Lincoln and others might be cited as examples of effective leaders who were given to melancholia, they were effective in spite of such. Not because of it.

That is not to say giddiness enhances leadership. It doesn't. Yet, a positive, upbeat attitude does. So, let's consider a few patterns of thought that, like a constant pursuit of happiness, might make us unhappy rather than happy.

One of these attitudes involves a failure to live in the moment. This reminds me of a story involving my maternal grandparents. Sunday lunch was always a treat at their house. It is one of my favorite childhood memories. One Sunday, as we were eating wonderful lemon meringue pie that my grandma had made for dessert, someone commented, "Grandma, this is sure good pie." Without a moment's hesitation, she replied, "Yeah, but it would be better if it was coconut."

After that, whenever my mother and I wanted a good chuckle, all that was necessary was for one of us to mention this incident. It was always mentioned, though, in a context of needless discontent.

The story has often caused me to wonder, if things are good or okay now, then why do I destroy the moment by wishing for something else? Why do I become preoccupied with yesterday's problems or with tomorrow's uncertainties? Put another way, why can't each of us just live in the moments which are perfectly fine? We would be amazed at how much happier such an approach would make us.

Another thief of happiness is the you-make-me-happy (unhappy) approach. This is where one is totally dependent on the actions or attitudes of others for personal happiness. With parents, this takes the form of being only as happy as your least happy child. For families, and from a similar perspective, we have the familiar line, "If Mama ain't happy, ain't nobody happy." A friend once told me a corollary to this: "If Daddy ain't happy, nobody cares." Yet, in spite of the intended humor in both statements, they point out a major flaw in happiness as it relates to all relationships—that happiness depends on others. It does not.

While others may contribute to happiness, others take happiness from us only through our consent. As legendary author and motivational teacher Zig Ziglar used to say, "Never put the key to your happiness in someone else's pocket."

Closely related to this is a third area of consideration. This says that we cannot be happy until circumstances are to our liking. An acquaintance once indicated this type of thinking regarding the economy. He tried to draw me into a negative conversation. As kindly as I knew how, I commented to him that I do my part when I vote, and that I choose not to worry about things I can do little else about.

"I can do something about it!" he nearly shouted.

"What might that be?" I quietly asked.

"I can protest!"

I indicated that we have that right, but that at some point, we have to just go on with our lives. He did not seem to get my point. I trust you do.

Someone has said, "Worry is like rocking in a chair. It gives you something to do, but it doesn't get you anywhere." When we can do something constructive—great! Worry, on the other hand, steals happiness.

LEADERSHIP TIP: Spend less time pursuing happiness and more time in worthwhile attitudes and endeavors. Happiness will find you.

Section Four: Other People Focus

Though we may bump into others by accident, we connect on purpose.

Let your light shine before men in such a way that they may see your good works, and glorify your Father who is in heaven.
– Matthew 5:16

A SMALL WORLD

I had just presented to attendees of the Independent Mystery Shoppers' Conference in Chicago. As I made my way to the back of the room for our scheduled break, I was greeted by a gentleman on the back row.

"Now I know where I know you from," he said. "I've been trying, for the past hour, to figure out where I've seen you before." Then he mentioned a public speaking course that I had instructed years ago. "That's it!" he said excitedly. "I was in one of your classes. You were my instructor!"

I couldn't believe he remembered me after twenty-five years. Actually, I thought that maybe he had me confused with someone else, because I sure didn't remember him.

"Really?" I asked excitedly. "Where are you from?"

"Pittsburgh."

I was disappointed. I wanted him to be right about where we'd met.

"I'm sorry," I said politely. "I instructed primarily in the Houston area. Never in Pittsburgh."

But, the gentleman persisted. "That's it! When I was in Houston on business I did make-up sessions there. You were the instructor!" Unbelievable!

This incident recently came to mind when a good friend told me her daughter and family attend church near our home, and that she was a member of the same church for thirteen years. Most people don't even know where Lavon, Texas, is. She not only knows but she has a longstanding connection there. It truly is a small world.

Perhaps it's not quite as small as a dear lady indicated in the San Antonio grocery store parking lot many years ago. She, a total stranger to us, noticed our Arkansas license plate and asked if we knew her daughter who lived in Little Rock, forty miles from our residence at the time. *Within reason*, it's a small world.

Having illustrated a common circumstance to which we can all easily relate, you might wonder concerning my point.

I would, first, make the point that since it is such a small world, our actions are not likely to go unnoticed indefinitely. Whether what we do is right or wrong, someone who knows someone who knows us will likely find out what we have done—and will talk.

If we are doing what we should be doing, that's great. If not, beware. Warren Buffet observed: "It takes twenty years to build a reputation and five minutes to ruin it. If you think about that, you'll do things differently." Beyond reputation, character says that regardless who might or might not see us, we will still do the right thing.

Another thing to keep in mind in a small world is that our influence for good or bad is greater than we think. During occasional periods of negativity, when I wonder how much difference I'm really making in the lives of others, I'm often humbled to learn that I made a significant difference in someone's life, totally unbeknownst to me and perhaps not even through direct contact. The same is likely true in your life as well.

All of this brings us to a type of challenge. As our world, through astonishing advances in technology, travel, and communication becomes smaller and smaller, our individual capacity and means for impacting others becomes greater and greater. Our job is to see that it's always a positive impact.

LEADERSHIP TIP: Your world gets smaller and your positive influence gets larger as you proactively serve others.

And He said to him, "'You shall love the Lord your God with all your heart, and with all your soul, and with all your mind.' This is the great and foremost commandment. The second is like it, 'You shall love your neighbor as yourself.'"
— Matthew 22:37-39

POWERFUL PEOPLE SKILLS

The fast-food restaurant that I frequent is located near our home. I've been going there long enough that the staff recognizes me as the fellow who always sits in the same booth.

Recently, while I had my head down reading, I heard someone trying to get my attention. When I looked up, I discovered that it was the manager. From behind the counter he held up a coffee pot and asked if I was ready for a refill. I couldn't believe it!

Long ago I had decided that the guy was just about the most unfriendly, unapproachable person that I had ever met. Whether he was just unhappy with his job or generally unhappy with life, I couldn't tell. His abruptness came across as one who had been weaned on a dill pickle.

One day I heard an employee call him by name. Just to be sure I'd heard correctly, I asked, "Did I understand him to call you Alex (fictional name)?" When he confirmed that I'd heard correctly and that it was his name, I started calling him by name. Thus occurred an amazing transformation from one who had previously acted like every coffee refill was deducted from his paycheck to one who thoughtfully asked if I was ready for a refill. It reminded me of the importance of names and of making others feel important.

Since this piece is not entirely about calling others by name (and remembering names), I'll share only one piece of information on the subject. This information is in the form of good news/bad news. Understanding that 37.5% of all statistics are made up on the spot, I have made up this statistic. I think it will not be far off: 90% of those who say they forgot a name didn't. That's the good news. The bad news is that they never knew the name to start with. So, they couldn't have forgotten something they never knew.

A German proverb says: "A poor memory has its roots in poor attention." Thus, when we meet someone for the first time we often forget the name because we weren't paying attention when the name was given. The most important technique for remembering a person's name is getting the name to start with, and then immediately starting to call that person by name. So, I asked Alex if that was, indeed, his name.

But I said that our subject is not entirely about names. It is, rather, about basic people skills—soft skills. In this regard, someone has noted "soft is hard." However, it becomes much easier when approached from a perspective in which we value others in the same way that we value ourselves.

For example, as use of our own names is a means of valuing ourselves (as opposed to being nameless nobodies), the same is true in the use of others' names. It's a way of showing that we value them. Other people skills demonstrate the same thing.

Courtesy works that way. Though "please," "thank you," "you're welcome," "excuse me," and similar expressions naturally come to mind at the mention of courtesy, other expressions of courtesy are also important. For instance, what about listening without interruption to what others have to say? What about focused listening rather than being consumed with thoughts of what we are going to say as soon as the other person quits talking or with checking messages on our phones?

In addition to how we value others through common (or not so common) courtesies, we also show that we value them by how we value their time. Have you ever noticed how much happier those folks usually are who show up late for an engagement, in contrast to those who are sitting there waiting for them to show up? We value our own time. Might others feel the same way about theirs? To value their time is a way of showing we value them. We do this by promptness, by limiting our requests involving their time, and by adding value to their lives by sharing worthwhile ideas—while they are sharing their time with us.

These are very simple people skills and perhaps, as you're reading this, similar skills come to mind. The fact that these skills are simple doesn't mean they're easy. However, when you consider that, more than anything else, people skills determine success or failure in life—it makes it worth the effort required to master these skills.

LEADERSHIP TIP: How much we value a relationship is demonstrated by how well we treat the other person.

"It is more blessed to give than to receive."
— Acts 20:34

HOW'S YOUR TRUST ACCOUNT?

As best I can remember, we were on a flight out of Albuquerque, New Mexico. I remember that the lady, the subject of this story, was from Albuquerque.

I was seated next to the window, and she was in the center seat. Having greeted each other, little else was said for a while. She was reading a book, and I did not want to disturb her.

When she took a break from reading and we both started munching on snacks, I decided to find out more about the attractive young lady who was reading the type of business book that I might read. Our conversation had not gone far before I became tremendously impressed with her. She was obviously articulate, knowledgeable, business savvy, and professional.

I asked her about her profession. She enthusiastically shared with me that she is the office manager for a large dental practice. She then described what they had been able to accomplish in terms of goals she had set and what she planned for them to accomplish in the future. She also said that she is big on staff development, which again indicated a lot about her professionalism.

While we were chatting, she casually asked me about my profession. Then she followed up with several great questions. In fact, the young professional was so good with her questions that she asked me one I am rarely asked.

Out of the blue, my new friend asked, "So when I'm talking to someone, how will I know if the person I'm talking to is a good fit for you in your business?" I was stunned! I had very early in our conversation figured out that my conversational partner was sharp. She had just told me *how* sharp she was. Enough about herself. She wanted to know how she might help me. I was blown away.

She had discovered one of the greatest connectors known to man: the ability to talk in terms of the other person's interest. And, while talking about my interest, she had indirectly sold me on herself, her ideas, and her services.

Her approach was not: "When do you plan to be in Albuquerque again? We're running a special on root canals, if you're having that sort of problem. Let me make you an appointment right now. Perhaps you are due for a cleaning?"

I've exaggerated for effect. Let's not miss the point. Even though she was wise enough, professional enough, and other-person-minded enough that she would never have said anything akin to my words, she made a sale. If I'm ever in need of a dentist while in Albuquerque, there is no doubt about who I will try to find. Yet, my friend had said nothing about getting my business. All that she said was essentially, "How can I help you in your business?"

It has been said that the number one reason people don't buy (us, our ideas, our goods or services) is because they don't trust the seller. While sometimes it may be true that the seller is not trustworthy, oftentimes lack of trust is because the seller hasn't yet established a trust account with that person. Talking in terms of the other person's interest is a huge deposit in this account.

LEADERSHIP TIP: Success comes from a giving, not a getting, attitude.

Be imitators of me, just as I also am of Christ.
— 1 Corinthians 11:1

A STORYTELLING HERO

It was a very busy, but incredibly good day in the Alamo City. It started *very* early. After looking over my speech notes and reading for a while, I stepped through the door of our adjoining rooms to enjoy room service and breakfast with my daughter. Amanda had accompanied me on the drive from Dallas.

Following our wonderful breakfast, I gathered up my things and took the elevator down twenty-six floors to the lobby of the Rivercenter Marriott. Shortly, my ride arrived, and I was whisked off to the meeting place where I did the keynote for a retreat of supervisors and managers for the city of San Antonio.

Following the presentation and after some rest back at the hotel, the incredible day continued as I met my good friend, Chris, for a light dinner. We had not seen each other in a few months and were eager to chat. Since we share similar interests, it was great to reconnect.

As we talked, Chris told me about a fascinating experience he and his wife had recently enjoyed. It involved a celebrity.

Chris said a friend called one day and asked if he and his wife would like to hear Rudy Ruettiger, of the movie *Rudy*, speak that very evening. After Chris said they would like that, his friend asked another question. How would they like to have dinner with Rudy before the speech? So, the two couples and Rudy had dinner together.

Rudy is quite a storyteller. So, I enjoyed immensely hearing Chris tell about Rudy's experiences.

One story especially caught my attention. In fact, it has been on my mind ever since Chris told it. The story involves a time when Rudy's daughter was asked to sing the national anthem before a Lakers game.

On game day, the family arrived several hours early in order to check out the Staples Center.

As they were looking things over, they noticed a lone player who was practicing shot after shot. "That's Kobe Bryant!" Rudy excitedly told his family. "I'm going to go out there and meet him." The security guards were not as excited about his idea as he was.

"No one interrupts Kobe while he's practicing," they said. "Oh, I'm not going to bother him," Rudy replied. "I just want to say hello." No way was he allowed on the floor.

Rudy came up with another plan. From the seats, he shouted, "Hey, Kobe, it's Rudy!"

Kobe stared in unbelief at the man behind the voice. "Rudy?" he yelled back. "Rudy *Ruettiger?*"

"Yeah," came the reply. "Rudy Ruettiger!"

In an immediate expression of profound admiration, Kobe walked over, stuck out his hand to Rudy, and said, "You are my hero!"

He then said that when he was a teenager growing up in Italy, basketball was not going well for him. Then one evening his dad had him watch the movie, *Rudy*, with him. To Rudy, his daughter, and his son, Kobe said, "That movie changed my life." A hero for many had met his own hero.

Perhaps neither Kobe nor Rudy are your heroes. I don't know who your heroes are, nor do I need to know. That is beside the point I wish to make. My point is this: heroes matter greatly, even to those who have achieved great things. In fact, many have achieved great things *because* they had certain heroes in their lives. Not only that, but because of their heroes, many have also been able to face some of life's greatest challenges.

My friend Chris is that kind of hero to me. We are both survivors of the same type of cancer. Several years ago, when this wonderful friend and oral surgeon found out I was scheduled to have the same surgery he'd had, he opened his heart and his busy schedule in order for me to pour out my intense fears and concerns and for him to candidly and compassionately answer all my questions. He inspired me with courage and hope. Though Chris' life has taken a different path from Rudy's, to me he is a hero simply because he cared enough to make a huge difference in my life. That doesn't require a big name—just a big heart.

Heroes come from all walks of life, but they have one thing in common: they all matter to others. We, each of us, matter to someone. We may not always know who that someone is. That doesn't matter. The Lord knows. What matters is that we *be* good heroes to others, and that we choose our own heroes wisely.

LEADERSHIP TIP: Be careful who you greatly admire, and be well aware that someone, somewhere greatly admires you.

And be kind to one another, tender-hearted.
- Ephesians 4:32a

KIND PEOPLE IN MOTION

It hadn't been a great week. The best part was a three-day visit from longtime San Antonio friends. We had such a great time! We spent one day at the world-famous, 1,000-square-mile flea market in Canton, Texas, buying things we didn't need but couldn't live without. Well, maybe not 1,000 square miles—but close. I've been there now, though Sherry might someday convince me once is not enough.

Other than the great time I just described (really!), on a scale of one to ten, the week had been about a three. Allergies that I thought had been left in San Antonio when we moved to the Dallas area, apparently made the move with us. They created a case of laryngitis that made speaking engagements an adventure. Plus, the medications I was taking left me feeling like someone had opened the top of my head and filled my brain with cooked oatmeal.

That week was also the week our son, Jon (USAF), was deployed to the Middle East. And, he, his wife, and son were on my mind and emotions.

So, when Sunday rolled around, I was spent. All I had in mind was to make it through the day without doing or saying anything unkind to anyone.

As per our Sunday morning routine, Sherry and I went to *our* restaurant for breakfast before going to church.

After we ate, for a little while Sherry worked the newspaper crossword and I read my Kindle.

Just before we got up to leave, two soldiers in uniform and a young lady were seated at a table near us. Thinking it a very small expression of appreciation for their sacrifices and those of their families, and with Jon fresh on my mind, I asked their waitress to give me their meal check.

What the waitress told me made me even prouder to be an American and to have a military son. "I already have three people who have asked for their check," she said with a smile. I was fourth in line!

Recently, following my presentation, a sweet lady commented during the Q & A on the lack of kindness we often see in the course of a day. I replied that many often scurry through life, while forgetting those around them. Then I told the restaurant story and pointed out that there are still a lot of kind folks in the world. We just have to look for them.

I had found some kind folks that morning, and I left the restaurant in a much better emotional state than when I entered. It made for a wonderful day. A mere exercise of the will would not have accomplished such a change in attitude, but positive *motion* did. Thus, a vital principle is once again established:

LEADERSHIP TIP: Though will power alone cannot change an emotion, motion can.

But Jesus called them to Himself, and said, "You know that the rulers of the Gentiles lord it over them, and their great men exercise authority over them. It is not so among you, but whoever wishes to become great among you shall be your servant."
– Matthew 20:25-26

MY UNFORGETTABLE DAY WITH BUZZ

Though it was years ago, I remember it well. My heart pounded with excitement. My hands sweated in anticipation. In an informal meeting with the speaker and his staff, we had carefully planned how it was to be done. Now it was nearly time for me, as conference emcee, to rush down the aisle and onto the platform. Lord, please help me to do this exactly right!

As the music on the eight-minute video rose to a climatic conclusion and the Apollo 11 emblem came on the jumbo screens left and right of the stage, the AV technician gave me the go signal. Taking long strides to the front of San Antonio's Grand Hyatt Texas Ballroom, I bounded up the steps and onto the stage. In a tone of voice that I hoped matched the emotional impact of the video, I excitedly said: "Ladies and gentlemen, Dr. Buzz Aldrin!" Five hundred people rose to their feet, in a thunderous ovation of pride and admiration. It will forever remain one of the most emotionally charged moments of my life.

During the days following the conference, and under calmer circumstances, I've done a lot of thinking. What I keep coming back to is what I might gain from the person who addressed the conference and the occasion with respect to leadership. Though many things might be said and a variety of ideas might be expressed depending on who is giving his or her perspective, three vital points come to my mind.

First of all, I came away from the event even more convinced that ordinary people are capable of extraordinary things. Understand that Dr. Aldrin and I did not become pen pals as a result of our brief meeting. Though I will remember him forever, who is to say how long he will remember me? Yet, even in our brief meeting I was able to observe some things that we had in common.

As emcee for the international conference, I wanted to do a great job. As our keynote speaker, he wanted to do a great job. We had that in common. I also noticed that he walked, talked, and even ate pretty much like I do. I saw him in the restaurant the previous night and was not even sure who he was, though I thought I knew. But, my point is that he was not wearing a Superman cape nor did he walk on water across the San Antonio River to get to the hotel. He seemed pretty ordinary.

His accomplishments make him extraordinary. Yet, he wasn't born with all "the right stuff." He became what he is by discipline and intense desire. I find that inspiring! We may not go to the moon, but everyone has within them seeds of greatness.

Additionally, Dr. Aldrin brought to mind something else about greatness and leadership: It all revolves around service. Unfortunately, many think greatness comes by reaching the top of the pyramid. In reality, it's the reverse. Servant leadership places you and me at the bottom of an inverted pyramid, and makes greatness dependent on the span of the pyramid.

Because of Dr. Aldrin's unselfish and courageous service, the span of his pyramid, in terms of the global and generational impact and contributions, is inestimable. His moon walk was truly a giant step for mankind and an enduring example of service for all leaders.

Finally, I must say that I came away from the occasion with a renewed desire to be a hero to somebody. On the stage that day, I saw not a pseudo hero but the real deal. Not a rock star, rapper, or some prima donna athlete, but someone worthy of admiration. We can be that to our spouses, kids, co-workers, clients, and friends. That's leadership at its best.

LEADERSHIP TIP: Aspire to be at the service end of the pyramid.

Give preference to one another in honor.
— Romans 12:10b

AIN'T FEELIN' IT

The legendary, late night talk show host Johnny Carson quipped: "Thanksgiving is an emotional holiday. People travel thousands of miles to be with people they only see once a year. And then discover once a year is way too often." Though a bit cynical at times and with respect to certain people, most of us have felt that way. The holidays and various other social functions throughout the year can provide ideal circumstances for being antisocial and stressed.

Familiar expressions like the following ones often reveal that there might be an issue in the making: "The holidays again?" "I sure hope I don't have to sit around and listen to (fill in the blank with the aunt, uncle, cousin, in-law, or outlaw) all day." "Do we have to go this time?" "Can't we just stay home?" "I'm not an extrovert." "I hate small talk." My personal favorite is: "I'm not being antisocial. Today I'm just not user friendly." I understand such thinking.

Dad used to say: "Terry was born tongue tied. So, when it came time for him to start talking, the doctor had to clip the membrane under his tongue, to free up his tongue. *And, he ain't stopped talkin' since!*"

That's not altogether true. By nature, I'm an introvert. I'm also a bookworm. A likely combination. With many years of consistent effort, I've trained myself to be an extrovert when I need to be, and also to engage in small talk when I need to. For many reasons, that's important. Not the least of these reasons is the one mentioned by Debra Fine in her marvelous book, *The Fine Art of Small Talk*. In it she says, "Small talk can lead to big things." So, whether you and I are at holiday gatherings or other social functions, we must keep in mind that as leaders (those with positive influence) it's important that we be sociable and that we talk comfortably with others, even when we don't feel like it. But, knowing and doing aren't always the same. So perhaps by keeping the following things in mind, we will be inspired toward action.

First of all, we should always remember that leadership is not a part-time role, no more than being a Christian is part-time. In other words, I cannot be a leader some of the time and a jerk the rest. Throughout the day, with family, friends, co-workers, strangers, or anyone else, a person of strong positive influence is consistently on. Otherwise, one's good influence is diminished, and his/her credibility is damaged. The only time a leader does not have to be *with it* is when he or she is alone.

Another consideration is that *everyone* matters, whether we want to spend time with them or not. They matter because they are people. But, they also matter because everybody is somebody's somebody. The person we may not especially want to be around is the son, daughter, father, mother, aunt, uncle, employer, employee, or coworker of someone whose opinion and respect we highly value and need. The fact that we might not see all of this at the time doesn't change the negative impact that we will discover when it's too late. Word travels fast—very fast in a high-tech world.

There is something else to remember. Mature people, while perhaps not approving of others' annoying habits or conduct, take into account their background and overall context. When we think about it, we have to conclude that the only reason we are not all rattlesnakes is because our parents were not rattlesnakes. That is just another way of saying that, given the identical background and circumstances of others, our attitudes and actions would be identical to theirs. Understanding that, we have an ideal basis for being more understanding and more considerate of those who are different. (Different is a more positive word for them than difficult.) We might even come to like them. Additionally, kindness creates a lot fewer problems than unkindness.

Let's keep one other thing in mind. It involves the price of being an effective leader. In one of my favorite movies, *A League of Their Own*, Tom Hanks said: "It's supposed to be hard. If it were easy, everyone would do it." Though he was talking about baseball, what he said applies very well to the soft skills of leadership. The reason many folks have little positive influence is because, in this case, soft is hard! These skills sometimes involve doing things we would rather not do. But, if the skills were easy, we would have no way of telling the true leaders from everyone else.

LEADERSHIP TIP: A major difference between real leaders and everyone else is that leaders often do things "they ain't feelin'" at the time. Also, while doing such things, they resist joining the immature who nobly suffer silently—while making sure the world knows they are suffering.

I have become all things to all men.
— 1 Corinthians 9:22b

HOW WE DRESS

In May of 2012, I received unplanned sleeping accommodations, compliments of Philadelphia International Airport. By that I mean I *had* to sleep in the airport. I felt fortunate for two reasons. First of all, it was a short night. I had arrived from a speaking engagement in Sardinia, Italy, at 11 p.m., and my rescheduled flight was to depart at 4 a.m. So, however uncomfortable I might have been, it wasn't for long. I also felt fortunate in the fact that it was the first time in all my travels that I had to sleep in an airport.

For frequent travelers, having to spend the night in an airport is not that unusual. It happens due to weather conditions, missed connections, and cancelled flights. However, what happened as I was making flight changes on this particular night was a bit unusual. It reinforced something that serves as the point of this story.

Since the flight I was on had been full, you can imagine the turmoil caused by everyone having to reschedule. The lines were to the moon and back.

As I moved toward the line at the ticket counter, I spotted a US Airways agent who was sort of directing traffic. So, I asked for his help. He directed me to one of the automated ticket machines and told me how to enter my information to book a new flight. The problem was that when I tried to use the machine, either I used it incorrectly or it was not working properly. So, I decided that I was about to spend the night in line in order to talk to someone at the counter.

As I walked back past the agent, to get at the end of the unbelievably long line for the ticket counter, he asked, "You get it taken care of?" When I told him I didn't and why, he said, "Come with me."

Next thing I knew, he and I were standing at the head of the line, in front of one of the agents at the counter. "This gentleman," he said to the young lady behind the counter, "has been waiting long enough. After the person you are now helping, he is next."

I had actually been waiting only ten minutes, or less. I was flabbergasted. I thanked him profusely, but could not figure out what had just happened. With time to think about the situation I think I figured it out.

First, I had treated him with utmost respect. Unlike some, I had not taken out my frustration on someone who was not at fault and was only trying to help.

But, I think there was something else at work. I think I had made a good first impression just by the way I was dressed. I looked like a successful business person, and not like someone who had dressed for a long night's rest on an international flight.

Please understand, what I just said is not intended to be self-congratulatory nor judgmental with respect to how others dress. It is simply to make a point that John Malloy, in *Dress for Success*, made many years ago. One is free to dress as he/she chooses. Others are free to choose how they perceive us by our dress—and they always do!

Ours is an increasingly casual society. Depending on the occasion, casual is fine. That said, consider this: Studies have shown that corporate productivity declines on casual Friday. What might that say? That our attitude tends to match our manner of dress?

Benjamin Franklin observed that if the whole world were blind, we wouldn't need clothes. His point was that we dress because others see us. That being true, then wise folks dress to show respect for others, and they also dress for the occasion.

I'm certainly not a fashion expert nor the authority on dress. In fact, about the only thing I'm certain of regarding fashion is that some handkerchiefs are for show and others are for blow. Regarding *people*, I know this: Anyone that I turn off by the way I dress is not likely to receive what I have to say.

LEADERSHIP TIP: Always make it a point to determine what will be the most appropriate attire for those who will see you.

Let your speech always be with grace, seasoned, as it were, with salt, so that you may know how you should respond to each person.
— Colossians 4:6

NETWORKING MAYBERRY STYLE

Every morning that I'm in town I have the same routine. At five o'clock I drive to a fast-food restaurant near our home, drink several cups of coffee, and read from my Kindle. Because I want to stay a size that allows me to fit through the door, I rarely have little more to eat than a single biscuit. Oh, and I also have a thin slice of heaven or, perhaps more accurately, a small taste of Mayberry.

You may think that's an exaggeration. It probably is. However, I look at it this way: Sherriff Taylor doesn't have to come through the door nor does an excited Deputy Fife have to accidentally discharge his gun for my mind to conjure up images of television's small town of Mayberry, from the 1960s *Andy Griffith Show*. I believe Mayberry is where you find it.

Seated at my usual spot, I'm afforded a peaceful, serene, Mayberry-like environment for planning my day, reading, reflecting, and watching the sunrise. I also get to watch people as our citizenry begins the day.

When we moved to our small town from San Antonio several years ago, I felt like an outsider. I could tell that folks wondered who the guy was who was sitting quietly, sipping coffee, and reading. They probably wondered, "What does he do?"

Then they began to warm up to me, as folks always do when we warm up to them. "Hello" and "Have a good day" soon evolved into short conversations, and those whose eyes were averted soon became friends.

I'm convinced that several things brought about this change in attitude. One of them has to do with the fact that to these customers I have never been a threat or intrusive—just kind. The other has to do with a friendly smile. I'm often reminded of something Phyllis Diller used to say: "A smile is a curve that sets everything straight." So, I've simply tried to help set their morning straight.

There is also the matter of names, and its impact on the change. When I sense that it will not delay these folks in getting where they need to be and during brief conversations, I make it a point to get their names. Then, during future visits, I call them by name.

For me, those things turn our town, or Anywhere, USA, into Mayberry. It's not a where. It's a who. It's not a place. It's people and relationships.

What I have just described is what is often missing in the popular concept of networking. Many seem to think that the key to business success is *just* formal networking. That is only part of the equation. The real key to business success is building relationships. If that can be accomplished through networking events, that's great. But it won't be achieved by simply swapping business cards and giving elevator speeches.

When I give someone in the coffee place an inscribed copy of my leadership book, it is because that person has become my friend. Someday that person, who perhaps works in a Dallas office, may become a client or may introduce me to a future client. That's great, but beside the point. Regardless of the business outcome, we'll still be friends. That's how it works, and I wouldn't want it any other way.

LEADERSHIP TIP: The key to life and business success is relationships, and relationships require consistent, conscientious, deliberate effort.

"Therefore be careful how you walk, not as unwise, but as wise, making the most of your time."
— Ephesians 5:15-16a

HOW TO GROW YOUR INFLUENCE

I love to have Rogelio, in the San Antonio J.W. Marriott, fix me up with a shoeshine when I'm in the Alamo City. He's the best, and I always walk out of there steppin' proud.

Another reason I like going to Rogelio is because I can identify with the work he does. A *very* long time ago I had a shoeshine stand in the downtown Riverwalk Marriott. It was a fun time, having a business on the Riverwalk and also having a chance to visit with folks from all over the world. But it wasn't all pleasure. Shining shoes is back-breaking work. So, I always tip Rogelio very well and walk away thankful for the memories—and another line of work.

Speaking of lines of work, I've had my share of professions as well as work-related experiences. Mind you, I've never been fired. Nor have I ever quit a job before I had another one. Early in life, Dad taught me that was usually not a very smart thing to do. However, in an effort to discover what I wanted to be when I grew up, I've barbered, preached full time, sold life insurance, taught a public speaking course, and sold emergency alert systems. Of course, now I write books and speak at conferences.

From each profession, I've gained an appreciation for the specific line of work and for those so engaged. I've also gained some valuable life lessons.

Though in a manner of speaking we're all in sales (at least of ourselves and our ideas), from direct sales I gained an appreciation for getting paid exactly what one is worth. No sale, no payday. Highly paid salespeople are very good at what they do. Salaried positions can be fine depending on the individual, but there are few things like a commission job to remind one that success comes through action—or failure through a lack thereof. But, really, I guess *failure to act spells failure* in most any endeavor.

And then there's professional speaking. Through it I've come to understand that different people like different things. At first, speakers are naïve enough to think everyone will be thrilled with what they have to say. If I didn't already know differently, I learned otherwise some years ago. Feeling good about the standing ovation I'd just gotten, I was brought back to reality when I read an evaluation form which said, "After three gongs, the hook should come out." Ouch! But no matter what we do, *we can't please everyone.*

Preaching can educate one to the fact that *people are people.* One tends to think that church people ought to be perfect. After all, practice needs to match faith, and I've found it usually does. However, when I'm inclined to believe a church member always has a certain wonderful quality, I then discover (as with other people) that sometimes he/she doesn't.

Along this line, as an instructor for the public speaking course I learned, as in no other profession, that we all have the same basic needs and fears. Doctor, lawyer, factory worker, salesperson, stay at home mom, executive, coach, or teacher—we all need to feel important and accepted. Furthermore, we're all afraid of failure or looking foolish in front of others.

Speaking of failure, writing can teach one *how to handle failure and rejection.* Since ninety percent of writers never earn more than ten thousand dollars from their work, the likelihood of making a lot of money from writing is very small. Yet, folks continue to write. It fills a need for expression. And, successful writers come to realize that prior rejection was not personal.

Barbering, though a dying art and different from anything else I've ever done, has a certain charm. Though it's certainly not the oldest profession, for centuries old-time barbershops have filled a need. They tie us to our past in a Norman Rockwell sort of way. They, and other institutions, give us a kind of *anchor amidst constant change.*

I suppose the main point one might get from these musings would depend on perspective. From this writer's point of view, it is this:

LEADERSHIP TIP: Greater roles of leadership, or influence, come to those who grow because of performance and experience in various roles.

Do nothing from selfishness or empty conceit, but with humility of mind let each of you regard one another as more important than himself; do not merely look out for your own interests but also for the interests of others.
– Philippians 2:3-4

RESPECT ISN'T TAXING

Every January it was the same routine. Because I didn't care to fill out all the necessary forms, I'd go to the state comptroller's office and have them figure the sales tax on books sold in connection with my previous year's speaking engagements. Then I'd write them a check before I left the office. It was not something I enjoyed. It wasn't the matter of paying that bothered me. It was just the idea of dealing with a bureaucracy—again. The experience always reminded me of Ronald Reagan's statement: "The number one job of a bureaucracy is to maintain the bureaucracy."

With the increase in book sales, I now let my CPA deal with my sales tax. However, I recall one January, back in the day. There was an added ingredient in the mix. It involved a new office location and unfamiliar agents. I was not looking forward to explaining why I had sales in various cities, and then answering various related questions. However, before entering the office, I sort of gave myself a pep talk regarding my attitude. In effect, I said: "Self, you're in the positive, upbeat, people business. Act like it!" I got no disagreement from "self" on this point. So I steeled myself and walked into the office knowing that things would go well.

As I entered the agent's cubicle, I stepped toward him and greeted him pleasantly. I immediately followed this with a warm handshake and my name. He seemed a bit stunned, but responded in kind.

As we went through the process of determining how much tax I owed, I began to casually chat with him.

"Mr. Smith, I guess this is pretty small stuff compared to some amounts you handle."

"Thank you so much for taking the time to figure this for me."

"Where do you call home?"

"Oh, you're from San Antonio? What high school?"

Though we graduated from different San Antonio schools, we were soon chatting like high school buddies.

Before long, he finished his calculations, and proceeded with the completion of the necessary paperwork. He then gave me the total figure, and I wrote out the check.

Once again, I thanked him, as we shook hands. All had gone exactly as planned while in the car, and I was pleased as I stepped to the cashier's window. Only two people were in line ahead of me, so the wait was brief. When it was my turn at the window, I handed the lady my check and that was that.

As I turned to walk away, I asked the lady if I might use their restroom. I was going to be out and about, and thought that might be a good time to use a clean restroom. As it turned out, their restrooms were not for public use. The cashier was nice, but definite in her refusal. I politely said that was okay, and turned to leave.

Then an amazing thing happened. Before I tell you what that was, permit me to ask a simple question: When is the last time you noticed a bureaucrat bending a rule for the general public? The answer to that question makes what I'm about to tell so refreshing and makes my new friend exceptional.

As I was headed for the door and my car, a gentleman's voice stopped me. "Mr. Sumerlin!" I turned to find that my agent had overheard the restroom request, stepped out of his office, and wished for me to follow him. He said nothing (other than initially calling my name), nor did I, as I followed him to the door in the back that was marked, "Employees only." He opened the door silently, and our eyes met. "You are very kind," I said with a smile. "Thank you so much." To underscore my appreciation of his caring attitude, I later went to the car, got one of my books, signed it, and placed it in his hand. He was touched by the token of appreciation.

As I later related this story to my longtime friend, Eddie, he pointed out that it was probably the first time a client had ever shown the man that kind of respect. My response was to ask why, in view of the positive attitude and goodwill that had been created, I don't always treat *everyone* as I had treated the agent.

LEADERSHIP TIP: Never underestimate the positive impact of genuine respect.

Respect what is right in the sight of all men.
– Romans 12:17

SO-CALLED BUSINESS ETHICS

Leadership is essentially positive influence. That being the case, never consider any interaction with others as meaningless. That includes children, perhaps especially children. I once had this lesson brought home to me as we were eating hamburgers with our daughter, Amanda, and her two little girls.

While we were eating, Amanda did something she has done for as long as I can remember. With delight, she touched a spot near her mouth to indicate I needed to use my napkin. It always annoys me when she does that. So, she has done it for years—for that very reason. She has been known to touch a spot even when I have nothing on my face.

To get back at her, when her back was turned, I stuck my finger in some ketchup and dabbed it on my forehead. (I know it was not very dignified and probably defies your image of me—or perhaps not.) When she turned around and saw what I'd done, we all had a big laugh.

Afterward we continued our conversation, until Amanda looked over at her youngest daughter. Unbeknownst to everyone, Lola (our little twenty-one-month-old at the time) had done *exactly* what Paca (their name for Grandpa) had done! She did it very quietly, yet with absolute confidence that it was the proper thing to do. After all, I had set the example.

We laughed, and then I thought: Paca had better be very careful. You had too! We had better be careful with *everyone*. Others notice, even when we think not.

In business, it's especially easy to forget that people notice everything. Sometimes we even think different rules and ethics apply in business, as opposed to other areas of life, and that no one notices.

I tend to agree with Peter Drucker that ethics is ethics. He said: "Business ethics assumes that for some reason the ordinary rules of ethics do not apply to business." Not only do they apply. They speak volumes about our overall character.

This came to mind some years ago when I took part in the 2011 Biz Growth Expo. I thought it was well promoted by the *San Antonio Business Journal*, well organized, and very productive. I thoroughly enjoyed the opportunity to connect with so many business professionals.

On another level, I was disappointed in what I observed in a few attendees. For whatever reasons, they apparently decided not to rent an exhibit booth. They, in effect, were roving booths. With business cards in hand (which is fine) and prepared mini sales presentations (not so fine), they became non-paying exhibitors. It seemed tacky and about as subtle as a hiccup.

Though not a problem to me personally, and certainly not something over which I had jurisdiction, it's nonetheless a problem. It's a problem of influence and ethics.

If a leader will cheat the system, what message does that send to his followers? What message does it send to potential customers? Personally, I feel that if someone will cheat the system he will also cheat me. It's clearly an approach that others notice and act upon.

LEADERSHIP TIP: Character leaks—into every action and interaction!

And whoever shall force you to go one mile,
go with him two.
– Matthew 5:41

THE SECOND MILE

Many businesses, for the present, can forget about second-mile service. They haven't gone the first mile yet. For them to proceed on the second mile would be like a child who hasn't learned to crawl trying to walk. It might be too big a challenge.

I witnessed this type of *service* on one occasion while standing in line at a fast-food place. It involved an unbelievable conversation between the fellow in front of me and the young lady behind the counter.

On this particular morning, I was standing behind the next fellow in line when I overheard the following conversation.

"Can you stir my coffee after you add the sweetener?" It seemed like a reasonable request. It wasn't anything like, "Could you walk barefoot on coals to bring it to me?" The request wasn't even labor intensive. So, the young lady's reply startled me. It was simple and to the point: "I don't stir it. I just put it in."

Admittedly, he was not in a five-star restaurant. But all he wanted was for the sweetener not to sit on the bottom of the cup. I've been there, as perhaps you have. Come on, lady!

Unfortunately, her job description didn't call for stirring before putting the lid on. You've got to be kidding.

That would be about like, when I barbered, cutting a customer's hair and then being asked if I would mind combing it before he gets out of the chair. "Sorry, I just cut it. I don't comb it." I wonder how long he'd be a customer and what kind of marketing it would take to win him back?

Such businesses can't blame the economy if they die. Cause of death would have to be hardening of the attitudes.

Conversely, I deal with a bank that believes in going the second mile with service. One day when I was too busy to walk across the street to sign a document, a new accounts person brought the form to me.

The ultimate display of their great customer service was in evidence on another occasion. At about 7 a.m., I was very busy when the phone rang. It was a teller at the drive-through bank next door. "Terry," she said, "you left your car lights on." As with the McDonald's incident, I was shocked—for an entirely different reason! Here's a lady who really cares.

Caring about people is the essence of great customer service and "loving your neighbor." It's the type of advertising you can't buy at any price. It's also a word-of-mouth method of marketing that spreads like wildfire. But for the necessary spark, we must have the right people.

LEADERSHIP TIP: Hire for attitude. Train for skill.

Section Five: Success

The main reason many never find success is they don't know what it looks like.

In everything give thanks; for this is God's will
for you in Christ Jesus.
— 1 Thessalonians 5:18

THE DISCIPLINED
PROFESSIONAL

Years ago, I asked a friend and corporate executive how many people he had working for him. "Oh, about half," he replied. His response reminds me of the fellow who was asked how long he'd been working at a certain place. He matter-of-factly answered, "Ever since they threatened to fire me."

Both anecdotes illustrate what is too often true: Many quit working as soon as they find a job! The question is why.

I'm not smart enough to know all the answers to that question. But I think I know some.

Some folks are just lazy. Some lose interest. Others are simply undisciplined. Perhaps they have good intentions that just never materialize. They fail to realize that success and reputation are determined by what we do, not by what we intend to do. They also overlook the fact that poor character is the result of poor habits.

All of the preceding leads us to the focus of this story: How can we have even greater discipline and better habits with respect to our professions? What might motivate folks to show up, do the work, complete the reports, provide the service, make the calls, build the relationships, take the training, and continue growing?

It would seem a positive perspective toward our jobs would be helpful to everyone. Along that line, please permit me to make three observations.

A job is a gift. By that I mean that something worthwhile to do and those who compensate us for doing it (be it providing goods or services) are priceless treasures that are not to be taken lightly. Can you imagine a life of nothing to do and no one to do anything for? I saw the personification of this, once, while on a speaking engagement.

One of the men in the group I was speaking to was in a supervisory position in the Texas correctional system. One day he took me on a tour of three prisons, which included lunch with the inmates in one of the prison cafeterias.

At one point on the tour, my host told me to follow him but stay close. He took me into the solitary block.

After we had walked a short way, he motioned toward a steel door with a small window at the top. "Take a look," he said. Seated on a mat on the floor was a young inmate. In the concrete floor was simply a hole that was used as a toilet. Except for a light that was on 24 hours, the toilet, the mat, and the young man, *nothing* else was in the cell. Nothing but time—to do nothing! I will never forget how I felt as I peered in.

If one doesn't like what he does, perhaps he should find something else to do. Until then be thankful, whatever your job, that you have something productive to do and someone to do it for. Have the discipline to do it well!

A job is invaluable. You might be saying, "That's obvious if you want something to eat or a place to live." True. But I have reference to the not so obvious.

Something useful to do is so valuable that it is inseparably linked to self-esteem. Often one of the best cures for low self-esteem is accomplishment, especially involving service to others. Charles Dickens said: "No one is useless in this world who lightens the burdens of another." Being paid for such service is not precluded.

Additionally, through honorable work, we contribute value to others. Shirley Chisholm said, "Service is the rent we pay for the privilege of living on this earth." If we can make a lasting contribution, then this rent bears compound interest.

A job can be easily taken away. All of us know some good person who has undeservedly lost their job. Unfortunately, it is a sign of the times.

On the other hand, consider this: A corporate retreat planner told me that the upside of a poor economy has been that many corporations have gotten stronger by having a means of letting people go who should have been terminated long ago.

Be not deceived! You and I can be replaced, and likely will be, if we choose the undisciplined approach to our jobs or professions. As a professional speaker, I can be replaced by someone who hones his or her speaking skills, does a better job marketing, does the research, and delivers a better product. Only discipline can prevent that from happening.

LEADERSHIP TIP: The best way to predict our professional future is to create it through discipline. (Adapted from Peter Drucker)

Whatsoever your hand finds to do,
verily, do it with all your might.
— Ecclesiastes 9:10a

HOW TO ACHIEVE

"Window seat, 30,000 feet, above the ground. Blue moon beams, on silver wings…" Those words sound like song lyrics, don't they? Actually, they are.

I was reminded of them in November 2014, as I stared out the window on the first leg of a flight to the island of Guam. There I conducted a leadership seminar for the wonderful folks of Guam Community College.

The early morning flight from Dallas to Los Angeles was nearly empty. So, in solitude I read, read some more, stared out the window—and did a lot of thinking.

Some might call it philosophical thinking. However, since Cicero said that there is nothing so absurd but that some philosopher has said (thought) it, I prefer to say I was engaged in a little common-sense thinking.

I thought of how I was actually doing what I had dreamed of and visualized for so many years. Every day, day after day, year after year, many years ago I listened to an old song by David Kresh. It contains the lyrics to which I just referred. I listened to the CD and pictured myself at 30,000 feet, traveling the world as a speaker. Weird, you say? Well, I figured I'd rather be weird and ultimately doing something I love, than not weird and spending a lifetime doing *anything* else.

The fact is that studies have shown *visualization* (of various types) not to be weird at all. It is a proven key to achievement. Put another way, there is power in dreaming with our eyes wide open.

There is also power in *patience*. Sherry might laugh at that statement coming from me, because I generally tend to be impatient. I tend to think that "patience" is two or more people in the care of a physician.

My brand of patience, though, is more along the line of perseverance. In that regard, I once commented to Sherry that I knew I was going to make it as a speaker, because I had already tried and discarded everything in the speaking business that *won't* work. But I had a dream, and the dream had me. So, impatience (quitting) was not an option.

Ignorance was also not an option. Will Rogers said: "Everybody is ignorant. Only on different subjects." I'm ignorant on many subjects. I often feel like the Louis L'Amour character who said: "The more one learns the more he understands his ignorance. I am simply an ignorant man trying to lessen his ignorance." The difference between success and failure, however, is in how much we are *trying to learn*—and use.

Though reading in our area of expertise is certainly important, something else is also important to learning. It's called our reference group, and it can determine up to 95% of our success or failure. It has to do with those we consider just like us.

If I might be permitted this personal illustration of what I just said, I will say that my career as a speaker took an upward turn when I started associating and sharing more with other professional speakers through the

National Speakers Association. If we are planning to achieve anything in life, it pays to frequently ask ourselves, "With whom do I associate and identify?"

One other thing came to mind as I stared out the window at the beautiful shoreline as we made our approach into Los Angeles International Airport. Though dreams are good, persistence is good, and effort is good; *single-minded focus* is a must for significant progress.

There is certainly wisdom in not quitting our day job while pursuing our dreams. However, I did not make significant strides in the speaking business until I sold a business I'd owned for many years, and began to focus just on speaking.

Serving "two masters" creates many challenges, not the least of which is fatigue, along with the fear and discouragement that often accompany fatigue. Eventually one has to, and does (sometimes by default), make a choice.

LEADERSHIP TIP: Dream big, but keep your eyes wide open through visualization, patience, association, and focus.

*(Love) bears all things, believes all things,
hopes all things, endures all things.*
— 1 Corinthians 13:7

GETTING REAL ABOUT OPTIMISM

Are you an optimist or a pessimist? Positive or negative? "Yes," you say? Good answer, because most of us are not entirely one or the other.

On the other hand, we have all run across those who are somewhat like the little old lady I heard about. She said, "I always feel bad, even on days when I feel good, for fear I'll feel worse tomorrow." It would be hard to say much that might help such folks. For the rest of us, perhaps some observations regarding optimism might be helpful in our daily lives.

First, let me say that a lot of junk has been said about optimism and a positive attitude. I suspect that I've said a lot of junk on the subject. Speakers often leave the impression that, with the right attitude, one can accomplish anything. That's not true!

Just suppose, for instance, that a very optimistic, non-athletic, six foot, fifty-something guy, suddenly decides to become a professional basketball player. Suppose he gets a professional basketball player as his coach, trains very hard every day and strongly believes in his goal. He even visualizes stardom and imagines that he can hear the roar of the crowd as he makes the game winning shot in the final game of the NBA finals. We know that no amount of work, visualization, or optimism is going to take him where he wants to go. Aside from size and lack of talent, the fact is that *young* men play professional sports.

Based on such, could we say that attitude doesn't matter? Actually, it not only matters, but there are times when it matters a lot to each of us.

For instance, it mattered a lot to me six years ago. That was when I had surgery for cancer. Believe me, I needed and wanted an optimistic surgeon.

Don't get me wrong. Optimism wasn't all I was looking for in a surgeon. But, answer this: Was I looking for a highly trained, eminently qualified surgeon who was *not* optimistic? I certainly didn't want to be operated on by someone who would say to me just before surgery, "Terry, I sure don't have a good feeling about this."

My point is that optimism doesn't equip or qualify one for anything he or she is not already qualified to do. Nor, by the way, does it change facts. However, it does equip one to do all the things one is equipped to do much better than pessimism.

That being the case, two things come to mind. The first of these has to do with how to maintain a more optimistic attitude.

To accomplish this, we must always be vigilant regarding what goes into our minds. Whether it involves what we read, hear from friends and co-workers, or listen to on TV, our thoughts are constantly being affected positively or negatively.

I like to say that I'm so optimistic that in our house we have snooze buttons on our smoke alarms. However, throughout the day, my mood can and does change very quickly, as a result of all the (mis)information we're subjected to. I'll bet the same is true for you. For that reason, we must all pay attention to our mind food. Junk food for the mind produces junky thoughts—which produce a junky life!

The other thing that comes to mind is how a positive, optimistic attitude toward people enhances our people skills. My author friend Geoffrey Tumlin has a formula that I like very much. He says, "Good communication = Good relationships = Good life." If communication is that important, what about the importance of having the right attitude toward people as a proper basis for communication?

People who like others, and who try to believe the best of others, convey optimism in conversation. That is true even in difficult situations. Conversely, those who are pessimistic and negative about life in general rarely have good communication skills, good relationships—or a good life.

LEADERSHIP TIP: Remember what the right attitude cannot do, but most of all, remember what it can do.

"And I was afraid, and went away and hid your talent in the ground; see you have what is yours."
— Matthew 25:25

D.A.R.T.ING PAST OUR COMFORT ZONE

I was not exactly paralyzed by fear. But I was *very* uneasy.

I had thought about giving it a try for a long time. After all, people of various ages, from all walks of life, use it regularly, and have for a long time. Major cities thrive on it. But I could not convince myself to check it out—alone.

I have given it a try with my wife, though. In such cases Sherry is always my navigator, someone I can depend on when the system makes no sense. With her, I know I will not get hopelessly lost.

What am I talking about? Metro type trains and subways. San Antonio, where I grew up and lived for 45 years, doesn't have such. And Lavon, Texas, where I now live, certainly doesn't have it (as well as a lot of other metropolitan type things). But nearby Dallas has DART (Dallas Area Rapid Transit). Along with other destinations, DART goes to the airports from areas all around the Dallas Metroplex. So recently, I got to thinking about the advantages of airport runs from the nearby town of Rowlett.

Sherry wouldn't have to deal with Dallas traffic to and from the airports (twice) to get me there and back. That's assuming I didn't drive myself to the airport, and then have to find a parking space. That can be a nightmare—and very expensive.

The train seemed the logical alternative. Logical, but scary. It's a long trip, with several transfers, involving lots of room for error. What if I miss my flight? Can't get to my speaking engagement on time? Am sued for breach of contract? Blackballed in the speaking industry? Our imagination can come up with all sorts of ridiculous things.

Finally, I put such thoughts and feelings aside and took the plunge. Sort of. One morning Sherry and I took the DART train and bus to Love Field Airport and back. We took the exact route I was to take in a few days, as a stress-free rehearsal for the real thing. Then, when the day arrived for my flight to Oakland, I was equipped with prior experience, along with a cheat sheet ("DART for Dummies") from my wife, to insure my success.

Though I was as nervous as a cat, it was a successful adventure. As my speaker friend Ron Hoesterey says: "Life is not a problem to be solved. It's an adventure to be lived." It was fun.

Without having to worry about driving in traffic, I tried to settle back and watch Dallas come to life, as we glided along at sunrise. What was once scary actually became a piece of cake.

What does all I've said have to do with you as a leader? A lot!

You see, everyone has fears that involve things outside their comfort zone. We must recognize such in ourselves and others.

Also, in the same way that my wife bolstered my confidence and helped me become more comfortable with a new situation, we all need help, and we can help one another to cope with life's challenges.

Additionally, my experience illustrates the need for a plan and experience (even rehearsal) to take on new challenges. Resultant success can help us build the confidence necessary for us to take on even greater challenges.

In my case, I felt confident enough that, after arriving in Oakland, I hopped on BART (Bay Area Rapid Transit), and explored much of Oakland and San Francisco. Did I know what I was doing? No! Was I scared? Yes! But I also had a great time.

Success not only has its own reward, in terms of confidence gained. In my case, there was an additional reward. True to what Sherry had written at the bottom of "DART for Dummies," when I stepped off the DART platform at the Rowlett DART Station, a beautiful woman *did* pick me up to take me home.

LEADERSHIP TIP: I completely agree with Helen Keller: "Life is a daring adventure, or nothing."

*"The Lord is my helper, I will not be afraid.
What shall man do to me?"*
— Hebrews 13:6

PARTNERING WITH FEAR

It was so weird. Though it happened in February 2013, I remember it as if it were yesterday. I was emcee in Scottsdale, Arizona, for an international conference.

The speaker was nearly finished. So, I started visually scanning the room for the next speaker. Normally that person could be found on or near the front row, with sort of a look of anticipation. My search did not produce even the slightest clue as to where the next speaker was.

The speaker at the podium finished his presentation. Applause followed, and then I anxiously waited for our next speaker to walk up to me. No one did. I stepped to the podium and asked, "Is Kim Lee (fictitious name) in the room?" She was not. So, I suggested that we break for a few minutes. I texted the meeting planner concerning the no-show and then franticly went in search of Kim.

As I opened the door to the meeting room, I nearly ran into an attractive, petite, soft-spoken, well-dressed, terrified young lady. Our speaker! We quickly exchanged names, I asked if she was ready (it seemed very doubtful), and we made our way to the platform.

Dana, the meeting planner, eager to find out what was up, had quickly arrived on the scene. Together, the three of us gathered at the podium and quickly got the PowerPoint set up for Kim's presentation. All the while, she looked like she might panic and bolt on us. Instinctively I gently took her arm, and asked, "Are you going to be okay?" She nodded affirmatively. I introduced her to the audience as a senior vice president for a huge, well-known bank, and sat down to wait for the other shoe to fall.

It was amazing! By far, she was the most liked and respected speaker of the entire conference. In fact, in the interest of time, we had to finally end her Q & A with the suggestion that those with additional questions touch base with her later. The audience could not get enough of her time and expertise.

Later, Dana and I laughed as we told the association president what had happened. "Terry even took her by the arm in an attempt to calm her down," Dana laughingly said.

Looking back, it is obvious that what happened in that meeting room is what often happens in life. First impressions lied.

Though it is true that we only get one chance to make a good *first* impression, it is not true that we only get one chance to make a good impression. Nor is it true that people are always as they first appear. Many friendships have been formed between those who at first did not even like each other. Conversely, immediate attraction has been known to eventually turn into abhorrence.

On closer examination, an additional thought surfaces from this strange story. Credibility counts, especially in communication.

I did not find Kim's presentation all that great. Of course, finance is not my field. Nonetheless, she was still not that great a speaker. But, she exuded credibility. She knew her stuff, knew that she knew it and all present knew that she knew it. Though small in physical stature, she is obviously a giant in her industry and also trusted. She epitomizes the concept that effective communication is more about what we are than what we say.

There is one other thing that Kim brings to mind. In many of our efforts, fear is our partner. Uninvited, it is nonetheless present. That is okay. When it is not okay is when our partner becomes our boss, and our creativity and dreams become empty wishes.

Later in our hotel room, when I told Sherry the Kim story, she said, "She is the lady I saw in the lobby. She looked like she was talking to herself. She was going over her speech." Indeed she was. She was also telling fear that it could come along, but that it would have to keep its mouth shut.

LEADERSHIP TIP: When it comes to fear, there is no substitute for solid character, knowing your stuff, and knowing who's the boss.

Do not be deceived, God is not mocked; for whatever a man sows, this he will reap.
— Galatians 6:7

LIFE'S CAUSES AND EFFECTS

Someone has observed that we are always free to choose, but we're not free to choose the consequences of our choices.

We see proof of this principle in Washington. The present state of the economy is the consequence of many years of bad fiscal choices. Recovery will depend on better choices.

Young people also demonstrate the accuracy of this same concept. Unfortunately, though they are free to sow wild oats, they have no choice regarding the crop with which they'll have to live. That's scary!

With respect to choices, they lack the wisdom of age which enables one to see the end from the beginning. Experiences, both our own and those shared by others, create this wisdom.

Presently, my concern is with how our choices impact various areas of our lives. What choices do we make that might yield unexpected and undesirable consequences?

I often jest that my career plan is to give my last speech after my 140th birthday, step off the stage, and drop dead of a heart attack. I enjoy speaking so much that I want to continue speaking as long as health permits.

However, even if my goal were realistic, an abundance of Blue Bell ice cream would likely keep me from reaching it. It is understood that no one is stopping me from choosing to eat as much ice cream as I want (and I *want* a lot). It is also understood that no one would stop the consequences from occurring, either.

I was close to a good man who indelibly stamped the validity of what I just said on my mind. After retirement, he chose not to exercise, and then to eat whatever he wanted in the amounts he wanted. He figured the doctor had a pill to fix everything. He figured wrong! The result cost him his life.

But health is not the only area where we can make poor choices. Many misuse their minds. The Internet is one means for such.

How we use the web is our choice. What we subsequently become by its proper use or its misuse is a result that is out of our hands. Too many forget that good people are the products of good thoughts.

Along the same line, we can't expect to sow nothing in our minds and reap something in our lives. In other words, it's not enough that one not misuse the mind. We must choose to use it.

Baseball great Satchel Paige said: "Sometimes I sits and thinks, and sometimes I just sits." He said *sometimes* he "just sits."

It's amazing the number of folks who "just sits" so much of the time—in doctors' offices, airports, hotel lobbies, restaurants, and on public transportation. Or, perhaps they're not just sitting but are on their favorite DTW.

"What's a DTW?" you ask. That stands for "designated time waster." In various meetings, the DTW would be the person who is designated to speak, but who wastes everyone's time by having nothing to say or by saying it very poorly. In our daily lives the designated time wasters can be electronic devices and/or social media. They can all serve very useful purposes (as can the Internet), but can also be mindless activities. Good reading or listening material, as well as stimulating conversation, are choices with far greater benefits.

Who we spend most of our time with is also a choice. It, too, is a cause we cannot separate from effect. Many have ruined their chances for success because of the one they chose to marry. Others have done so because of their friends and mentors. Because we ultimately become the effect of what our associates and our brain food cause, it's very important that in both areas we make wise choices.

LEADERSHIP TIP: If the effect is something we do not want, consider that it's likely the result of a cause we did want. Choose again! Choose wisely!

And He said to them, "Beware, and be on your guard against every form of greed; for not even when one has an abundance does his life consist of his possessions."
— Luke 12:15

THIS THING CALLED SUCCESS

Many years ago, I planned to own a Major League Baseball franchise. No. My name is not Nolan Ryan. At the time, I was simply pursuing a business dream that I thought was going to make me an incredible amount of money. It did make me one thing. Broke!

That venture, along with a number of other failed ventures, put me on not-so-friendly terms with bill collectors and the IRS. Receiving a phone call was an adventure—would it be a friend, an opportunity, or someone demanding money we didn't have?

So, I've long been in favor of having money. (Even a lot of it would be fine.) It certainly relieves the stress caused by not having money. It also increases options. And, as someone has said, "Whether you're rich or you're poor, it's nice to have money." However, money's not the whole picture.

It's been my privilege to have a few friends with enormous amounts of money. I've noticed that, contrary to what we might think, money doesn't shield them from life's troubles such as family problems, health issues, heartache, disappointment, fear, and insecurity. In fact, money can sometimes compound such problems. I've also noticed that wealth tends to magnify the strengths and weaknesses one already has. In other words, there are some extremely good, generous people who are rich but there are also some wealthy, super classless jerks.

What I'm saying is that I no longer see money as a sure indicator of success or a lack of money as an indication of failure. Money is basically a reward for what one provides and a tool for doing good or evil.

In view of this, I think I am over any craving I ever had for a lot of money. Sherry and I, though not having a lot of money, are thankful that we're comfortable.

From a different perspective, career goals as they relate to success can often be as challenging as riches. For instance, for a long time I thought a bestselling book would be the mark of success. Then, in 1997, my bestselling, first book came out. At least, in my mind it was a bestseller.

It was such a big hit that I invited myself to do a book signing tour in all the major book markets: Lubbock, Midland, Odessa, and Amarillo, Texas. I drove 1,400 miles, did three radio interviews, three TV interviews, and four Barnes and Nobles—all in one weekend! I sold three books. That was not three in each store. That was total! One of the sales was to our son-in-law's parents in Amarillo.

Since then my books have done well. I wonder, though, was I a failure when they weren't selling well? How many would I have to sell to be a success?

Then there's the matter of fame. When I did enrichment lectures, it was cool when, after I'd given my first presentation of the cruise, passengers would recognize me around the ship. Now, as I travel about, I'm occasionally recognized because of my speaking and writing.

There was also the time a few years ago when I was emcee for the ATM Industry Association's US conference in Scottsdale, Arizona. For a day and a half, I had the attention of 1100 attendees. The very thoughtful meeting planner even put me in a palatial resort suite for a couple of nights.

Those expressions of special treatment help me forget about times like the one many years ago when, at a hotel on the San Antonio Riverwalk, I did a presentation for a speaker's bureau. I was so awful that the client complained to the bureau. Ask me if the bureau ever booked me again.

My point is this: Whether we're talking about money, achievements, a little fame, or the nice things in life, it's all pretty iffy. So, what really matters concerning success and leadership?

Since I believe leadership to be positive influence and success to be positive relationships, please permit me the following anecdote. It involves a leadership presentation I did for the Social Security Administration in Albuquerque, New Mexico.

I arrived on a Southwest red-eye the night before the engagement, right after speaking in Dallas and San Antonio. I was running on fumes. However, when I got to the meeting room the next morning, the meeting planner had a nice surprise for me. She said that a nice fellow from a previous engagement was present.

Before speaking, I spotted the young man in the crowd and walked over to greet him. He rose, we shook hands warmly, and he looked me in the eye. "You changed my life," he said. "I lost my father two months before you spoke at our meeting. I was a wreck. You turned my life around."

The audience didn't know that I was just given all I needed to refuel and to give them 200%. About midway through the presentation, I told them, "I speak because I believe that somewhere, sometime, I might be able to help someone in some way." To me, THIS is success.

LEADERSHIP TIP: Success is not what we get or possess. It's what we are and how we use it.

*And let not your adornment be merely external;
but let it be the hidden person of the heart, with
the imperishable quality of a gentle and quiet spirit,
which is precious in the sight of God.
−1 Peter 3:3a, 4*

WINTER PHOTO OP

"**I**f that picture shows up on Facebook, you're in a lot of trouble." That's what I jokingly told Priscilla, our daughter-in-law, several Christmases ago.

"That picture" is the same one that became their screen saver. It's also the same picture that our son, Jon, laughed at every time he walked past their computer.

Priscilla took the picture when we were visiting them one winter. Taken in their front yard on Tinker AFB, near Oklahoma City, the photo shows Jon and me in our snow-shoveling outfits. We were clearing fourteen inches of the white stuff off their driveway.

Jon looks fine. He's tall, youthful, well built, and properly attired. I, on the other hand, forgetting for the moment the tall, youthful, well-built stuff, will simply say I was not properly outfitted. The only items I wore that looked stylish were my leather jacket and the smartphone hanging from my belt.

Though my trousers were Dockers, they were conspicuously tucked into the tops of Priscilla's boots with the frilly fur around the tops. They looked very un-Docker like. But, I figured Priscilla's boots would work better in the snow than my loafers, despite how her boots made me look. Besides, the borrowed ski cap that hung rather loosely on my head looked to me more ridiculous than the frilly boots. But, who cared? The thought never crossed my mind that I was dressing for a photo op.

As I looked at the picture on the computer screen, what I disliked most about it was not the boots or the ski cap. It was the fact that, dressed as I was, I looked like my father. Mind you, there was nothing wrong with Dad's looks. However, I like to think I'm young and he was… Well, you know what I mean.

Suddenly, while we were discussing the picture, I came to realize that Jon had an entirely different take on the photo. Though the picture made him laugh, what he saw wasn't simply someone who was ridiculously dressed—or even someone who looks like his grandfather. Though I can't recall his exact words, I do remember that he expressed how he felt about the picture in a very touching way.

As I was jokingly raising sand about their embarrassing screen saver, Jon finally said, "Dad, I love that picture! To everyone else you're all serious. (I took that to mean I'm a professional and am often seen in coat and tie.) But, to me you're just Dad."

At this point you might expect me to say that success without the respect of those we love is empty. While that's true, the point of our story goes much deeper. So, that we don't miss it, here it is:

LEADERSHIP TIP: When you strip away the titles, roles, accomplishments, and appurtenances of so-called success, what remains—remains longest.

Therefore…be steadfast, immovable, always abounding in the work of the Lord, knowing that your toil is not in vain in the Lord.
– 1 Corinthians 15:58

STAYING THE COURSE

"You must feel like the cruise director on the Titanic." Those words were whispered in my ear by a well-meaning attendee at the back of the room, moments before I strode to the podium at the conference for the Automotive Trade Association Executives in New Orleans. I chuckled grimly because I was well aware of what he was talking about. I had been telling myself for months that the very last thing I wanted to do was come across as some sort of wild-eyed optimist.

My concerns were confirmed when, minutes before my presentation, the group was told that the National Automotive Dealers Association reported over 900 dealership closings for 2008. I could hardly ignore the elephant in the living room. Nor, as I told them, could we do anything about it.

Then and now the economy and the struggles of various industries are external uncertainties. At that time, I wanted to address some certainties in effective leadership that would help all of us to weather good times and bad. Perhaps you can benefit from these same solid leadership constants.

1. *Real enthusiasm.* Zig Ziglar used to tell of standing in line for a table in the hotel restaurant, the morning following his speech the previous night. "There's our

speaker," one lady whispered to her friend. "He doesn't look very motivated this morning," was the reply. Zig said that he often wondered how you stand motivated or enthused.

I fear we have confused enthusiasm with excitement. Excitement generally depends on circumstances, is superficial, and is temporary. Enthusiasm, on the other hand, has little or nothing to do with circumstances. It is fire in the belly. It's a belief in the Lord, ourselves, our people, our cause, our goods, and our services. It triumphs over circumstances and often makes them better.

Real leaders have real enthusiasm regardless of what might be going on around them!

2. *Contextual awareness.* Successful leaders constantly monitor the ever-changing contexts of their followers. The following story well illustrates this need:

A man and his wife returned from dinner and found a thief standing in their living room. "Oh no," he said. "Now I'm going to have to shoot both of you so I won't have any witnesses." He turned to the lady and said, "You're first." Then, as an afterthought, he asked, "By the way, what's your name, lady?" "Elizabeth," she sobbingly replied. "Oh no! I can't shoot you," he said. "My mother's name was Elizabeth." Then, turning to the man, he said, "But I can shoot you. What's your name?" Haltingly the man replied, "My name's Bill, but all my friends call me Elizabeth!"

Few men want to be called Elizabeth. However, circumstances might change that desire a bit. Effective leaders understand that stress and desperate circumstances might cause followers to do all sorts of uncharacteristic things. While such might not be a valid excuse for poor attitudes and actions, real leaders pay close attention to context.

3. *Positive persistence.* If one is digging a hole and it keeps filling in, mere persistence is not what's needed. What's needed is the use of some other type of digging equipment or to find some other place to dig a hole. Similarly, "positive persistence" is just another way of saying wise, yet optimistic persistence.

My friend Paul (not the one in this book's dedication) epitomized such positive persistence. He told me some rather startling facts about his new project. He said that he had planted an olive grove near Pearsall, Texas (just south of San Antonio).

I was surprised to know the Pearsall area is good for olive trees. I was also startled to know he had planted 10,400 trees and that he'd hired an expert and foreman out of Dallas. Most startling of all, though, was when he told me he would not get his first crop for three years. You see, Paul started his project at 91 years of age. Most fellows at that age don't even buy green bananas. Yes sir! Paul planned to positively persist with his olive grove and with the matter of living.

LEADERSHIP TIP: True leadership qualities never change with circumstances.

But the wisdom from above is first pure, then peaceable, gentle, reasonable, full of mercy and good fruits, unwavering, without hypocrisy.
— James 1:17

HOW TO BE A "BOSS"

There is a wonderful story involving the days when Larry Bird played for the Boston Celtics. K.C. Jones was the coach.

There were five seconds left in the game. They were tied with Seattle, and it was Boston's timeout. In the huddle, Bird said, "Why don't you just give me the ball and tell everyone else to get…out of the way?"

Jones replied, "Larry, you play, and I'll coach." Then Jones called the play, "Kevin, you get it to Larry, and everybody else get…out of the way."

Who is the real leader in this situation, and who is the boss? While I'm not trying to say K.C. Jones' coaching style was that of a boss, on this occasion he was the boss. Larry Bird, on the other hand, was the real leader. We readily see the difference. My question is: Which are we most of the time, and how can we tell the difference?

One common way we can tell the difference is in the way bosses think regarding what they know. Bosses tend to know everything. Of course, it's obvious that no one really does. Bosses, however, want to leave the impression that they do.

Sometimes what they think they know is expressed as if it's a divine oracle. Along this line, I recall a description that some preacher friends of mine had concerning a mutual preacher friend: "When he's wrong, he's gloriously wrong." However, in his mind he was never wrong, and when he spoke it was always with utmost authority. This type of person has often been described as having a concrete mind—all mixed up and permanently set.

The other side of the coin on this point involves the frustration that is felt by the boss when he/she finally discovers they don't have the answer. While leaders humbly say, "I don't know, but I'll find out," bosses often beat themselves up when they must admit they don't know something. Or they just fake an answer, which can create huge problems. First of all, it's not honest. Second, in an age of smartphones, others can easily look up the facts almost before we can get the misinformation out of our mouths. So, to reiterate, we can tell bosses from leaders, oftentimes, by how they deal with what they don't know.

Another characteristic of bosses is that they generally are adamant get-it-doners. This trait can be good in terms of the obvious (getting things done). It can be bad because of its close kinship with impatience and inaccuracy. Because of impatience, the get-it-done person tends to swap what could be great for what *might* be good enough, just to get it done. Likewise, patiently doing it right the first time is swapped for having to do it over. Both typically disregard relationships, because the number one issue to the boss is just to *get it done!*

One more observation is that bosses tend to be short on humility and long on ego. Someone has wisely observed that E-G-O stands for Edging God Out. I think that pretty well sums it up.

Christian leaders understand that the I-A-N, on the end of the word Christian, reminds us that without

Christ I Ain't Nothin'. Therefore, we pray for the Lord's help every day, so that we can be the kind of leaders He would have us to be in all that we say and do. He is the vine. We are the branches. We're nothing without Him!

LEADERSHIP TIP: Christian leaders know who the real leader is.

*In speech, conduct, love, faith and purity show
yourself an example of those who believe.*
— *1 Timothy 4:12b*

WHAT IS A REAL LEADER?

For over twenty years, I've been writing and speaking on leadership. I suppose you already knew that, though, since I'm the only one who has ever dealt with that subject. Actually, the very opposite is true. It would be impossible to imagine how many have addressed, and do address, the subject of leadership. That being the case, I make no claim for knowing everything there is to know on the subject. I'm also reasonably certain that there have been times when I (as well as others) have spoken nonsense in the name of leadership.

Given all that, I've been thinking a lot about what life's experiences and associations have taught me regarding outstanding leaders. It has been my privilege to be associated businesswise and socially with some of the best.

Since I tend to be a noticer, what did I see in such individuals? What did I learn from them that might be of help with respect to the positive influence known as leadership?

Though the following three characteristics obviously are not the sum total of what defines a leader, in my mind they take precedence over many other qualities that might be on a long list. I hope you agree.

At or near the top of my leadership list would be solid values. Leadership guru, Peter Drucker, said: "Management

is doing things right. Leadership is doing the right things."
Effective leaders do not waffle on the "right things," nor
do they reset their values every time they are tested by
wants and pressures.

Many years ago, a fellow speaker and friend told me of
a call he received from an executive of one of the largest
corporations in the country. His conversation with the
gentleman well illustrates my point.

At a time when my friend needed the income, the executive on the phone, based upon what he already knew
about the speaker, made an incredible offer. His company generously offered to sponsor the speaker's career!
There was only one problem. There was a large issue in
the speaker's mind regarding being associated with that
company's products. He declined the offer, and for his
courage he has always had my admiration.

I'm sure that others could have rationalized and talked
themselves into doing what they really wanted to do.
However, as Tom Selleck said, in his *Blue Bloods* role as
police commissioner of New York: "A funny thing about
decisions: You don't seem to need to talk yourself into the
right ones."

As surely as effective leaders demonstrate their solid
values, they also are known as people people. This means
more than a large number of social media friends. It means
solid relationships and consistently positive influence.

Few illustrated this better than my friend, George
Wenglein. He and his brother-in-law, Robert Luby,
founded Luby's Cafeterias. They both knew how to treat
people and, thus, were widely respected. They were both
customers back when I owned my barbershop.

I remember something that I saw George do many times toward the end of his life. When he was too ill to drive and had a driver, he had the same routine every time he was brought to the shop. Once he was situated in the barber chair, he would give his driver cash and instructions to go get donuts for his barber friends.

Here was a man who could barely walk because of illness. Yet, in spite of his own physical challenges, as a people person, he maintained a cheerful disposition and was mindful of others. He was a giver—not a taker. And, he built an enormously successful business and life through that approach.

The third quality on my short leadership list is vision. Vision is contagious! Effective leaders know that. They also realize that leadership that is of the greatest value is the kind that will outlive them. So, they enthusiastically mentor, inspire, assist, and invest in those who will carry their vision forward.

I once read about two men who attended the graveside service of a mutual friend. One of the attendees was ninety, the other ninety-five. As they turned to leave, the ninety-five-year-old quipped to his friend, "Ain't much point in us going home." I don't relate that to be macabre. I tell it only in recognition of their candor and to encourage us to face the inevitable at any age. Because of that inevitability, we need a vision that will outlast us.

I know a couple whose vision, in part, involves helping young people to become successful. For that reason, when the man and his wife learned that a promising young waitress was working hard to put herself through college, they decided to fund *all* her education. Perhaps we are not that financially capable. Yet, we are all (as parents, grandparents, professionals, community leaders, and role models) capable of doing what we can with our talents, time, expertise, and funds.

Most have heard of Sir Christopher Wren and his architectural creations, the greatest of which is the rebuilding of London's Saint Paul's Cathedral following the Great Fire. On the church crypt, where Wren is buried, a huge blue plaque bears these words: "Reader, if you seek his memorial, look all around you."

As surely as architecture is a memorial to the genius of Sir Christopher Wren, effective leaders bespeak the influence of those who knew what leadership *really* is.

LEADERSHIP TIP: Never underestimate the power of your influence or the certainty of the living memorial that people will see as they look all around.

MAY I HELP?

You may have noticed that, though the book has the word "Christian" in the title, nothing has been said about *becoming* a Christian. The book has been entirely about *being* a Christian every day.

Please do not take this as an indication that I believe becoming a Christian is unimportant. It is very important!

If I may help you in understanding what is involved in becoming a Christian, I would be honored to do so. You may e-mail me at terry@terrysleadership.com. Let me also urge you to read *The Gospel According to Luke* and *The Acts of the Apostles*.

To subscribe to my free leadership newsletter, please go to www.terrysleadership.com

Other Books by Terry L. Sumerlin

Available at Amazon.com

Leadership: It Takes More than a Great Haircut!

A Human Becoming: A Life Changing Voyage

Barber-osophy: Shear Success for Your Cutting Edge

Barber-osophy: Hair We Go Again

*Also available for your favorite E-reader

CPSIA information can be obtained
at www.ICGtesting.com
Printed in the USA
FSHW021756130819
61012FS